CREATIVE
ZENDALA ANIMALS

An Adult Coloring Book
with Positive Affirmations

Transcendental
Coloring

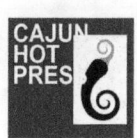

CAJUN
HOT
PRES

I APPRECIATE MY UNIQUENESS

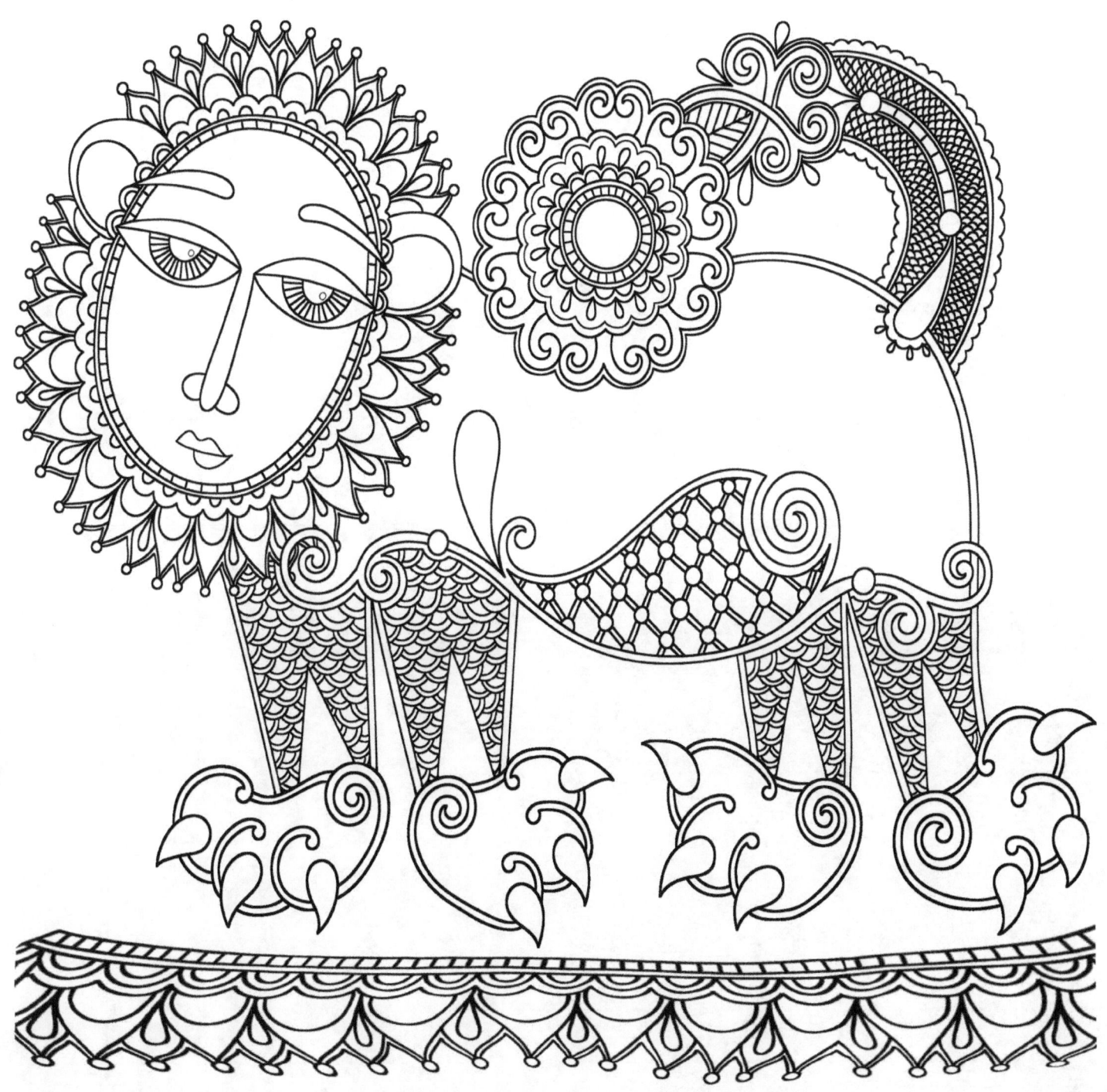

I EXPRESS MYSELF

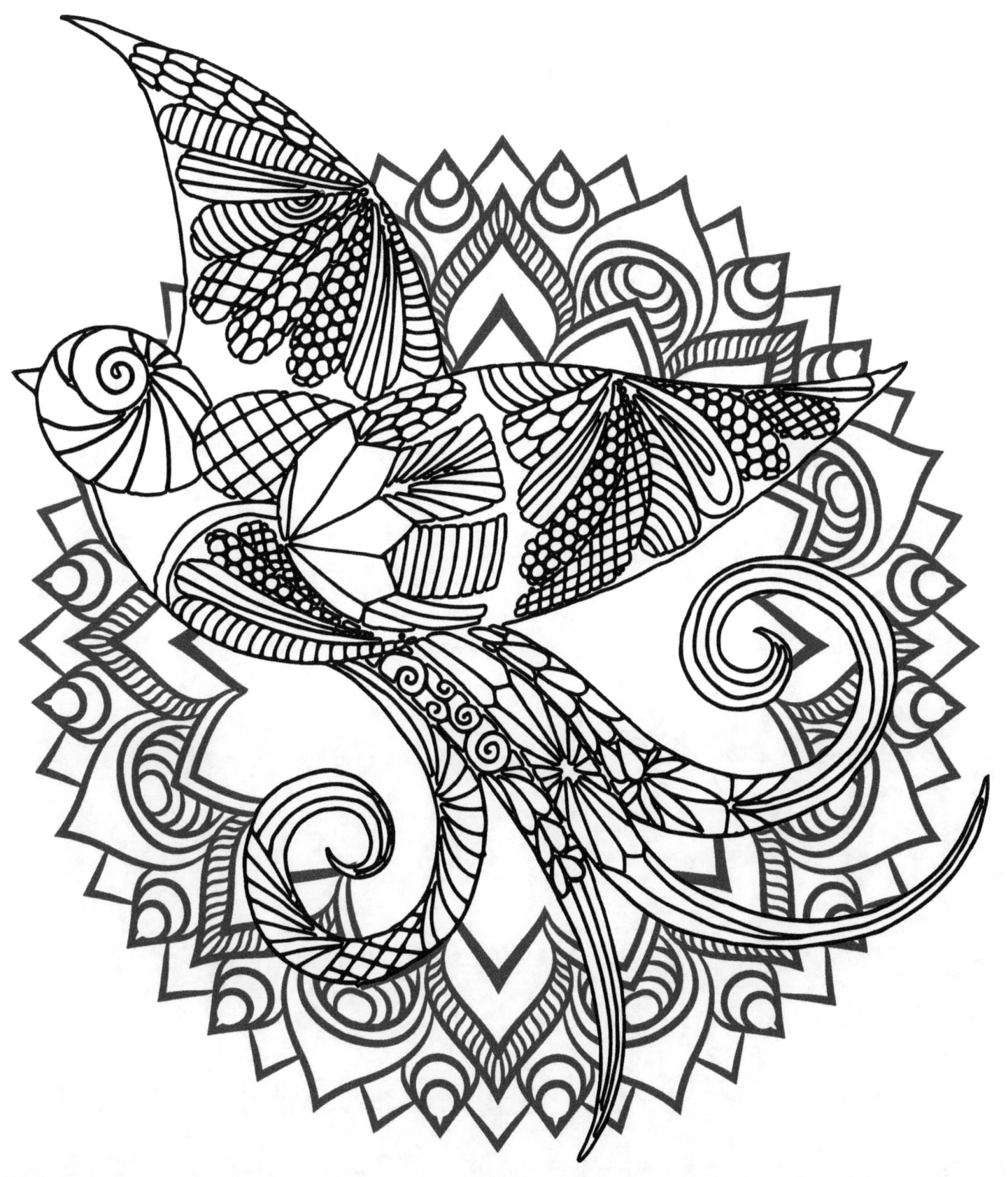

I AM COLORFUL

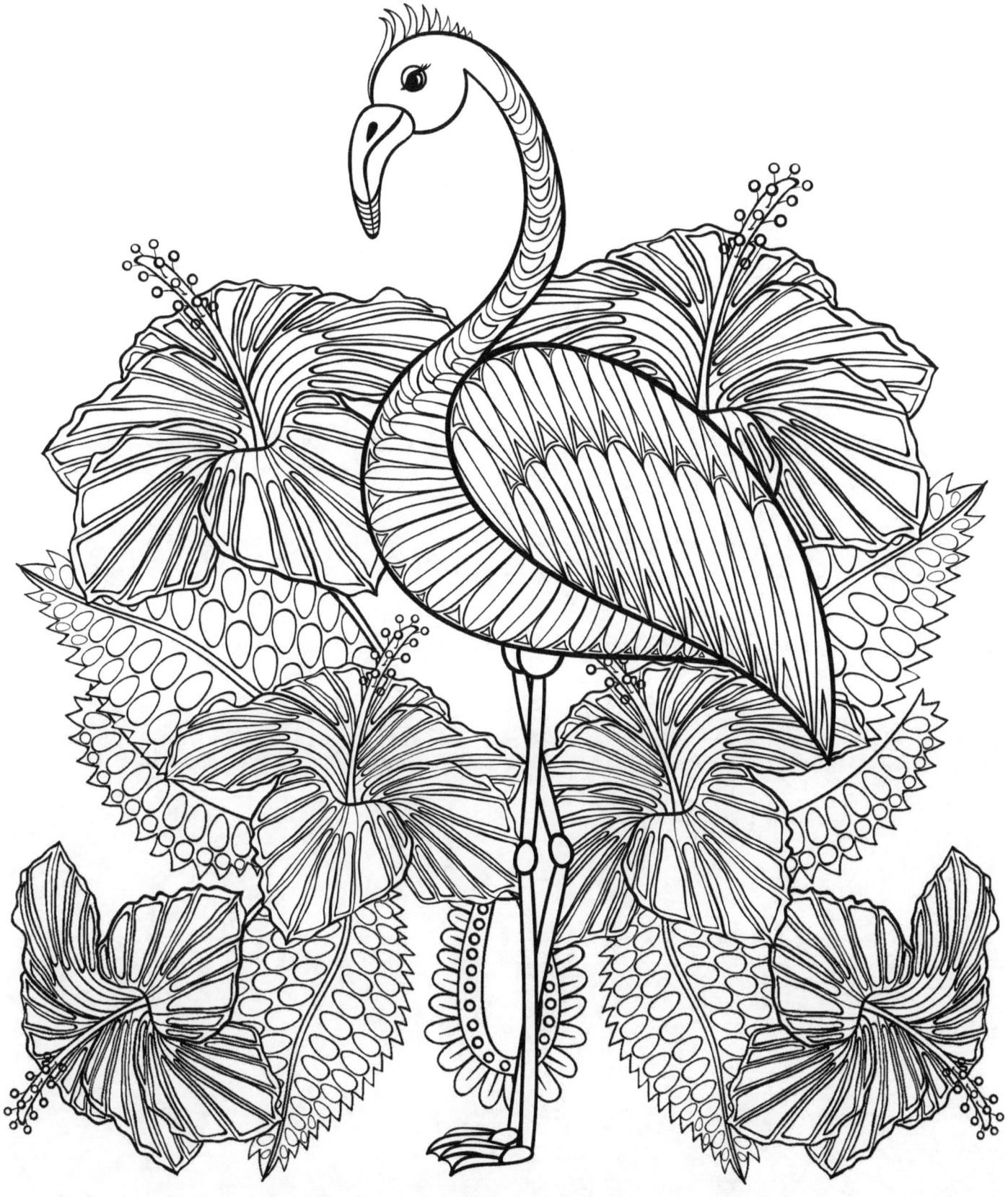

I AM FOCUSED

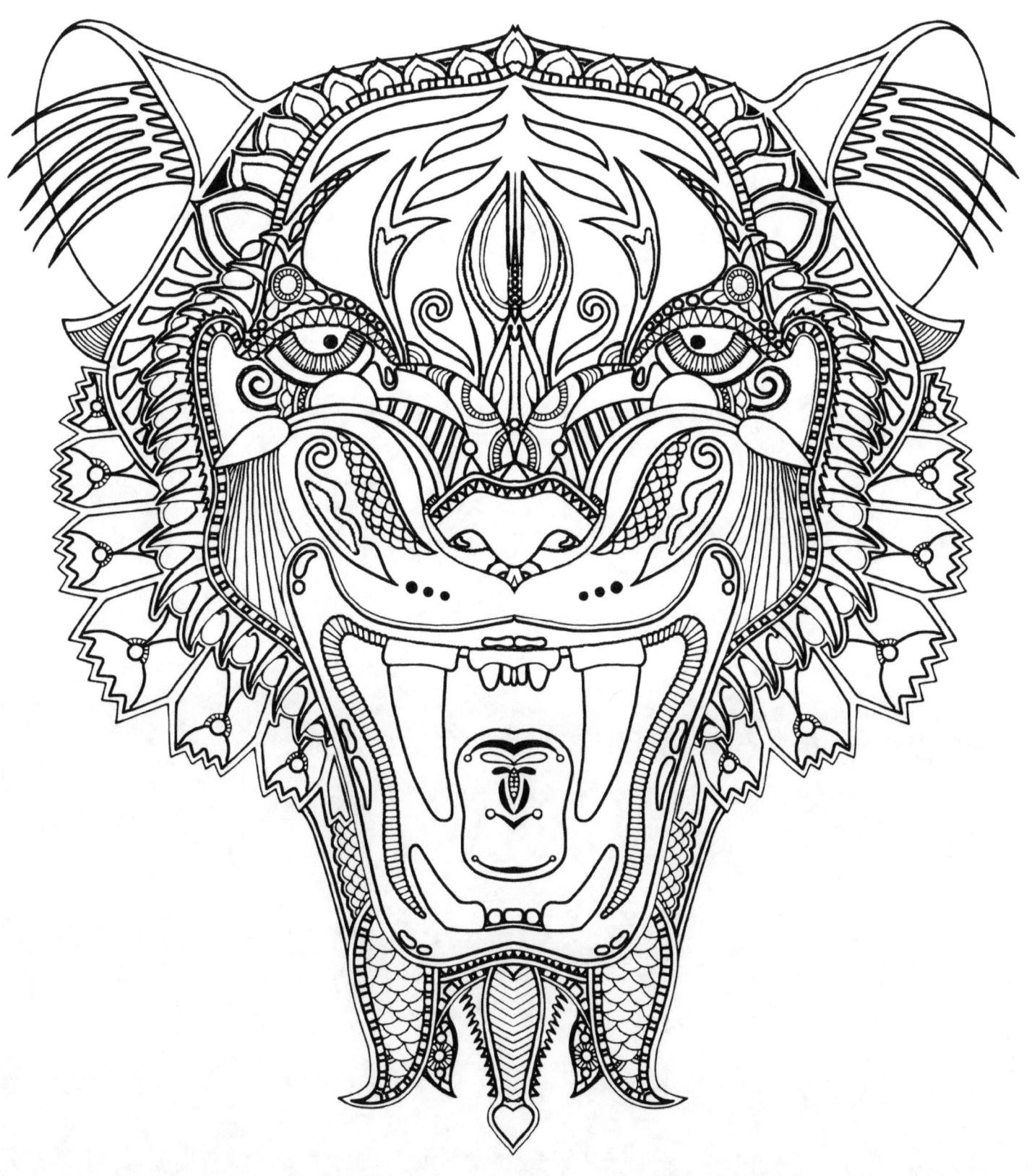

I AM A QUICK LEARNER

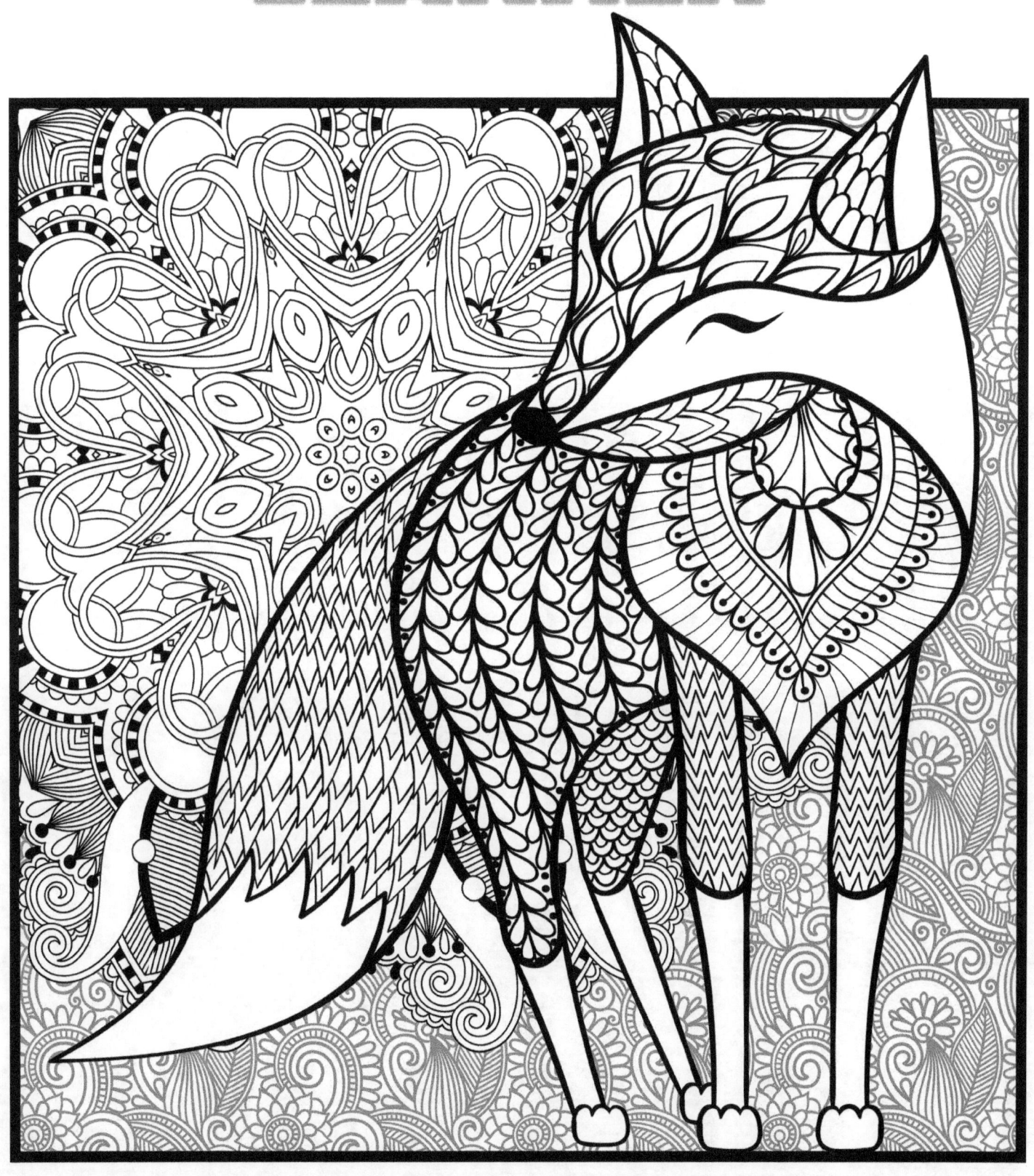

I EAT WELL

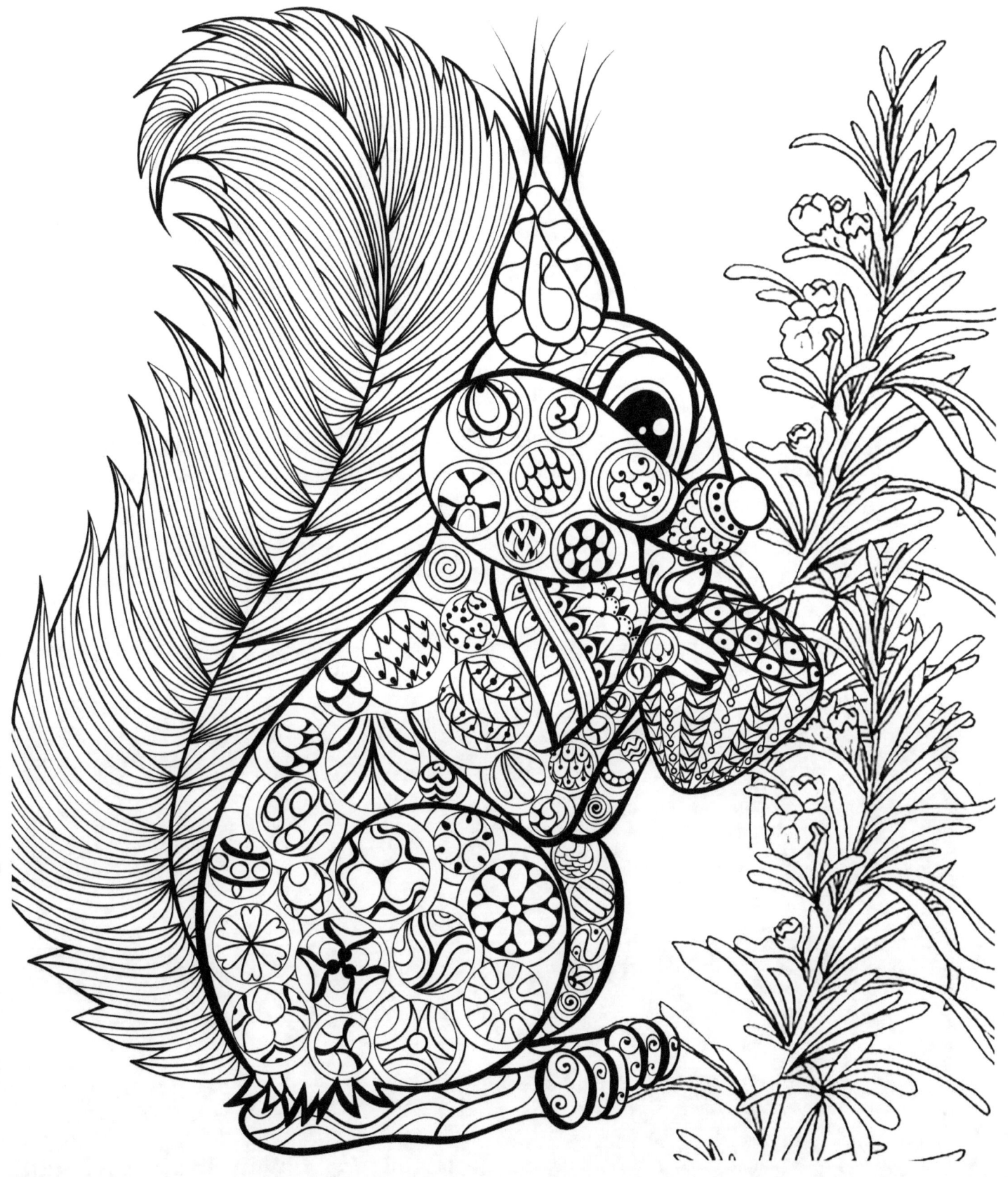

I FORGIVE MYSELF FOR MY MISTAKES

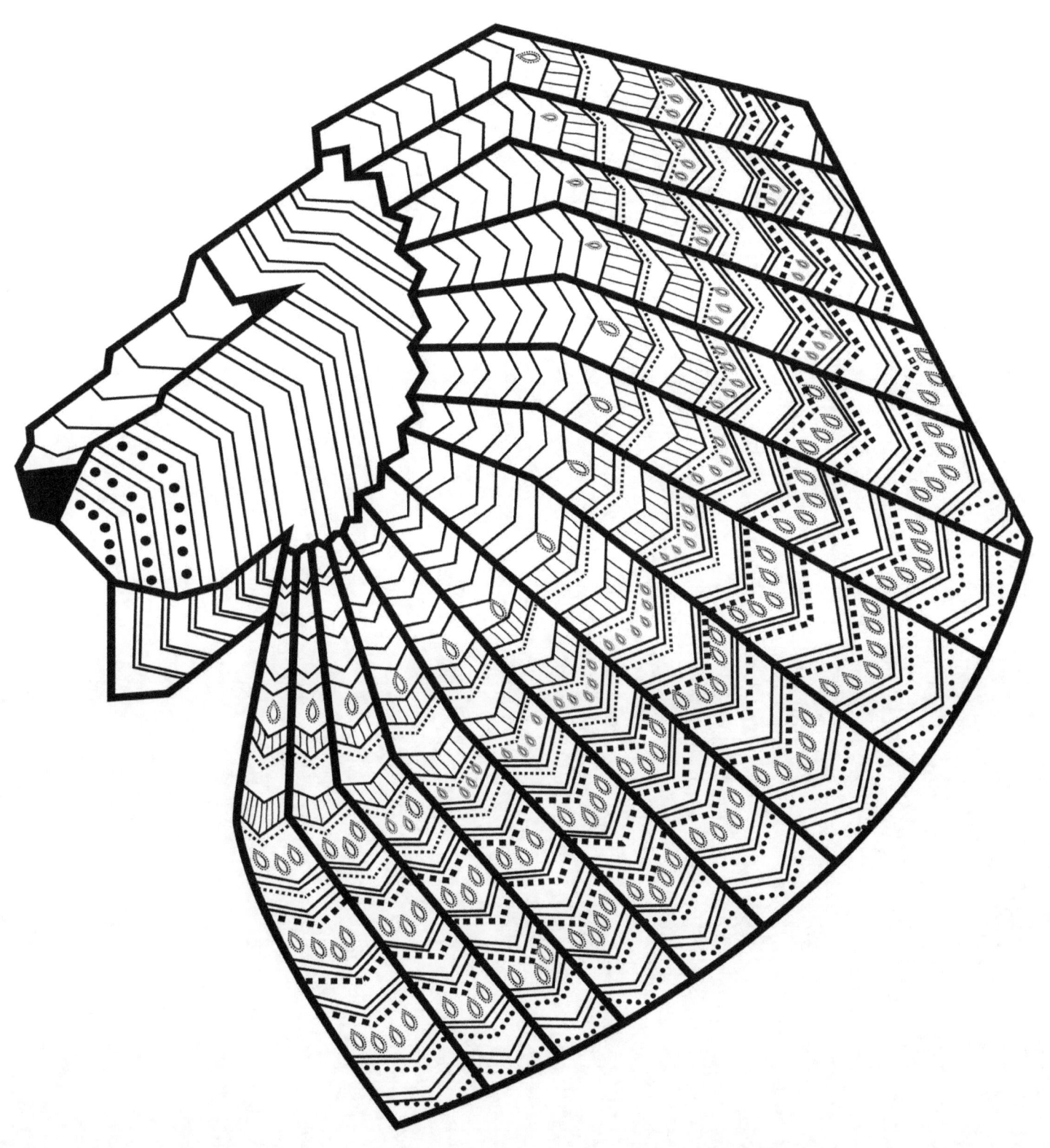

I AM DOING THE VERY BEST I CAN

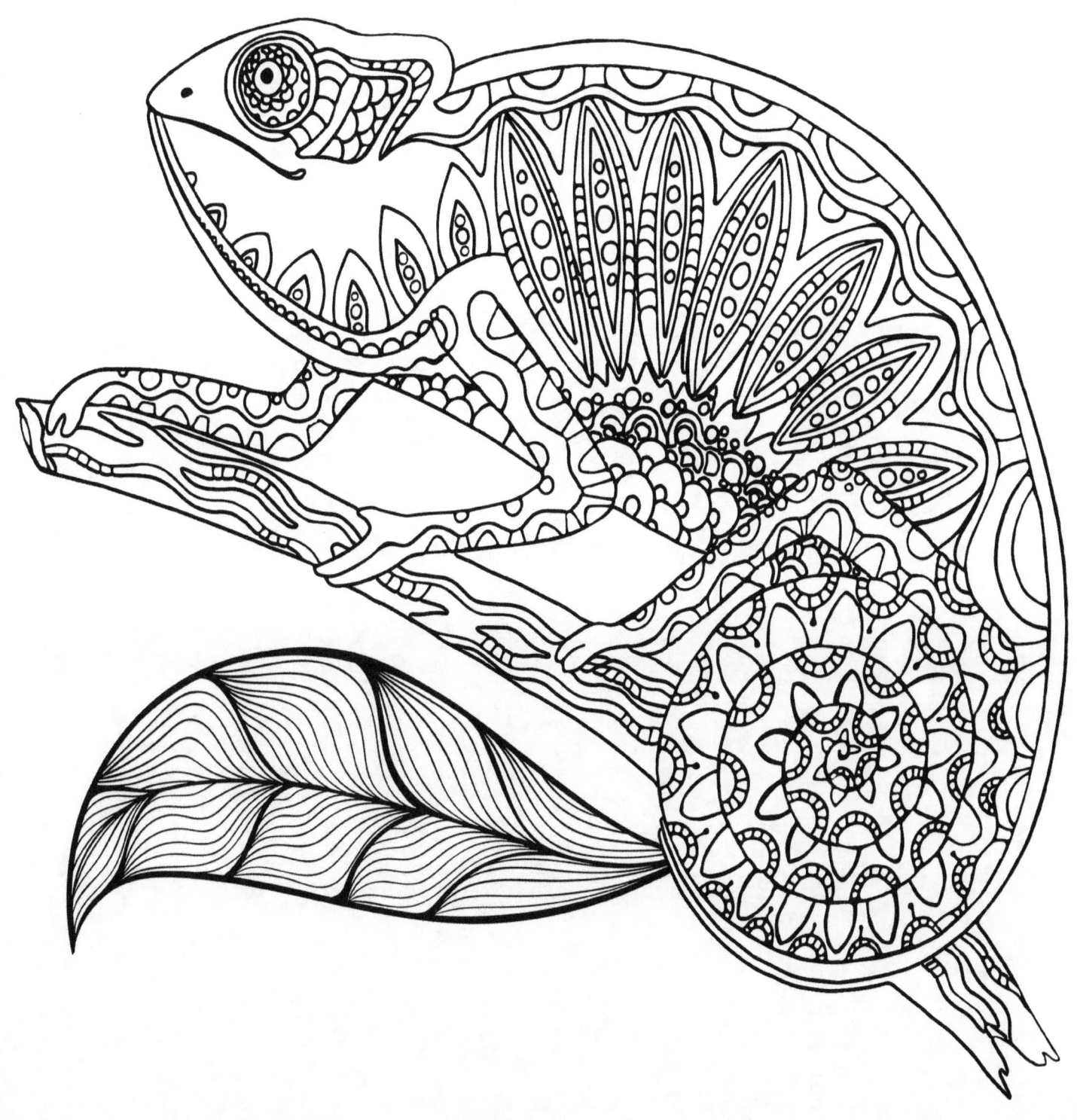

I APPRECIATE MY PHYSICAL BODY

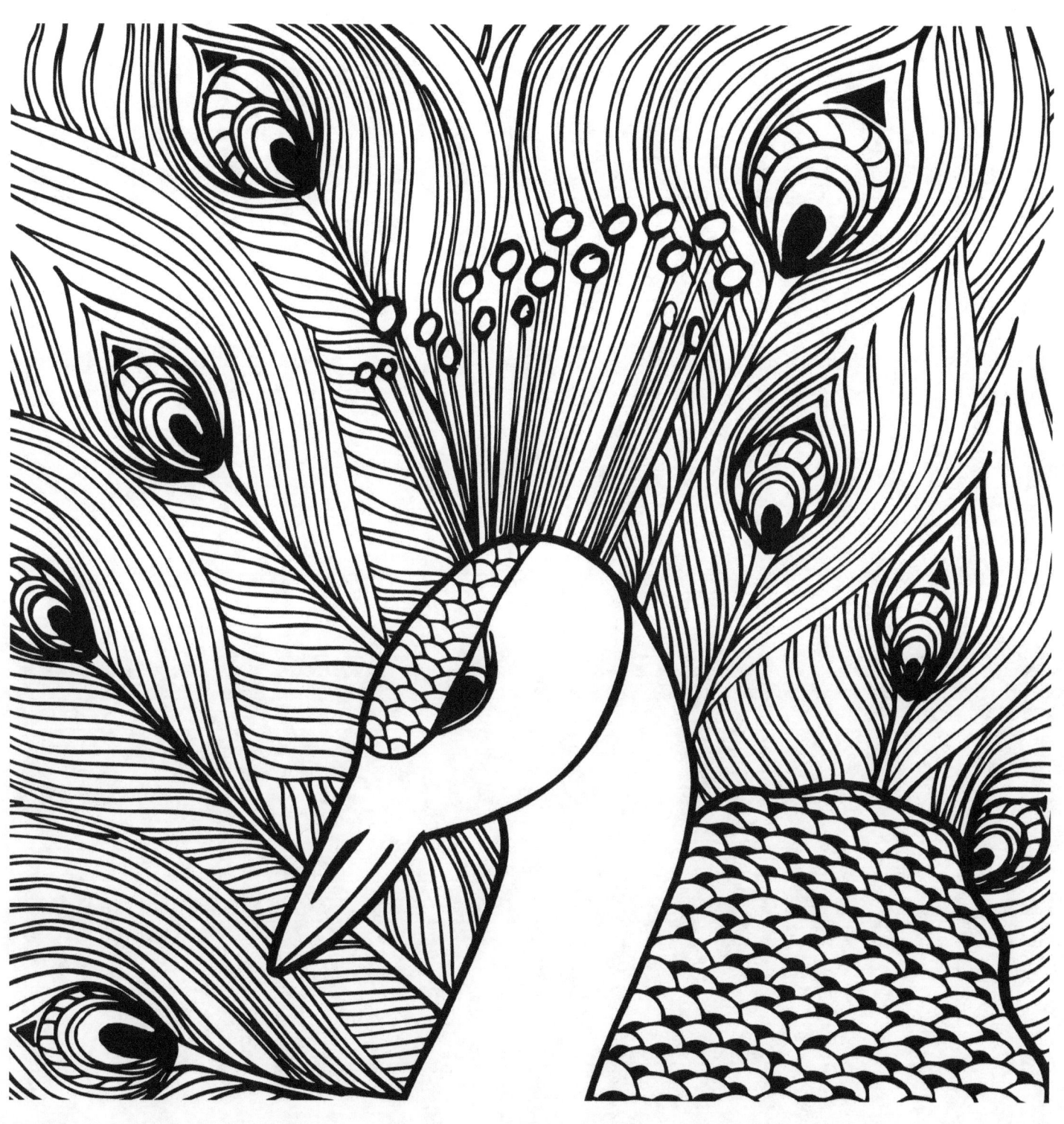

I HAVE FREE WILL

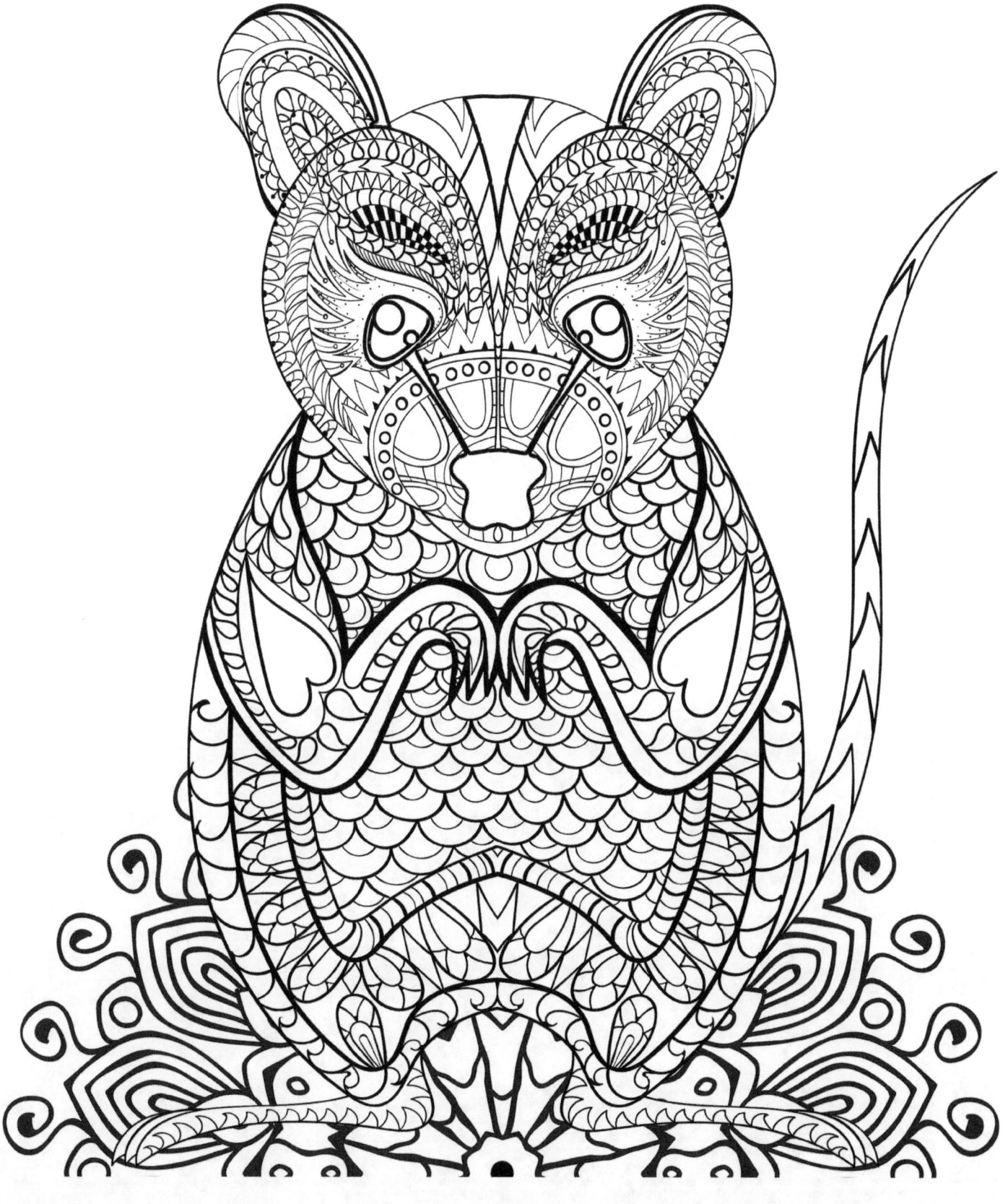

I LET GO OF THE PAST

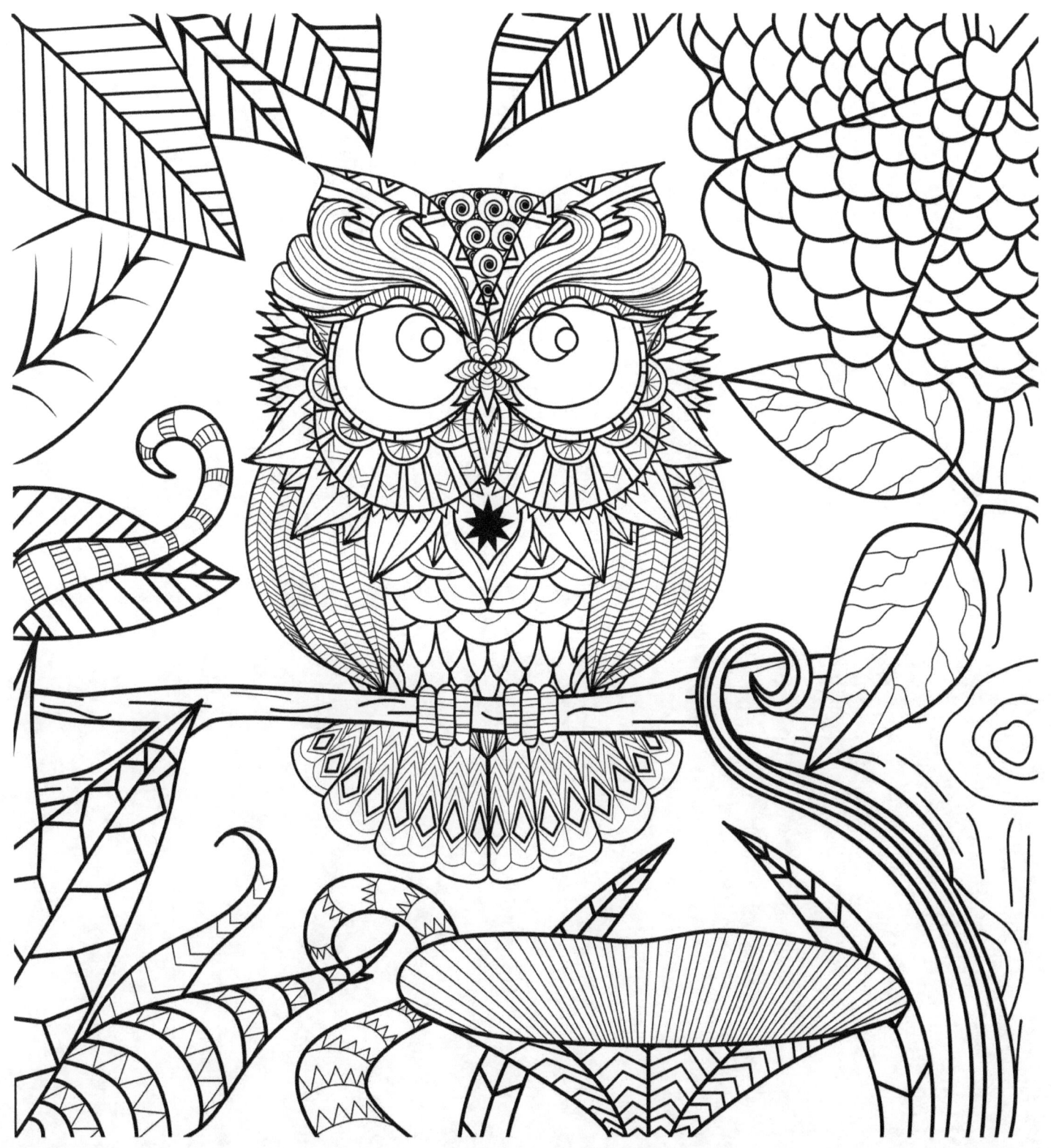

I ENJOY MY RELATIONSHIPS

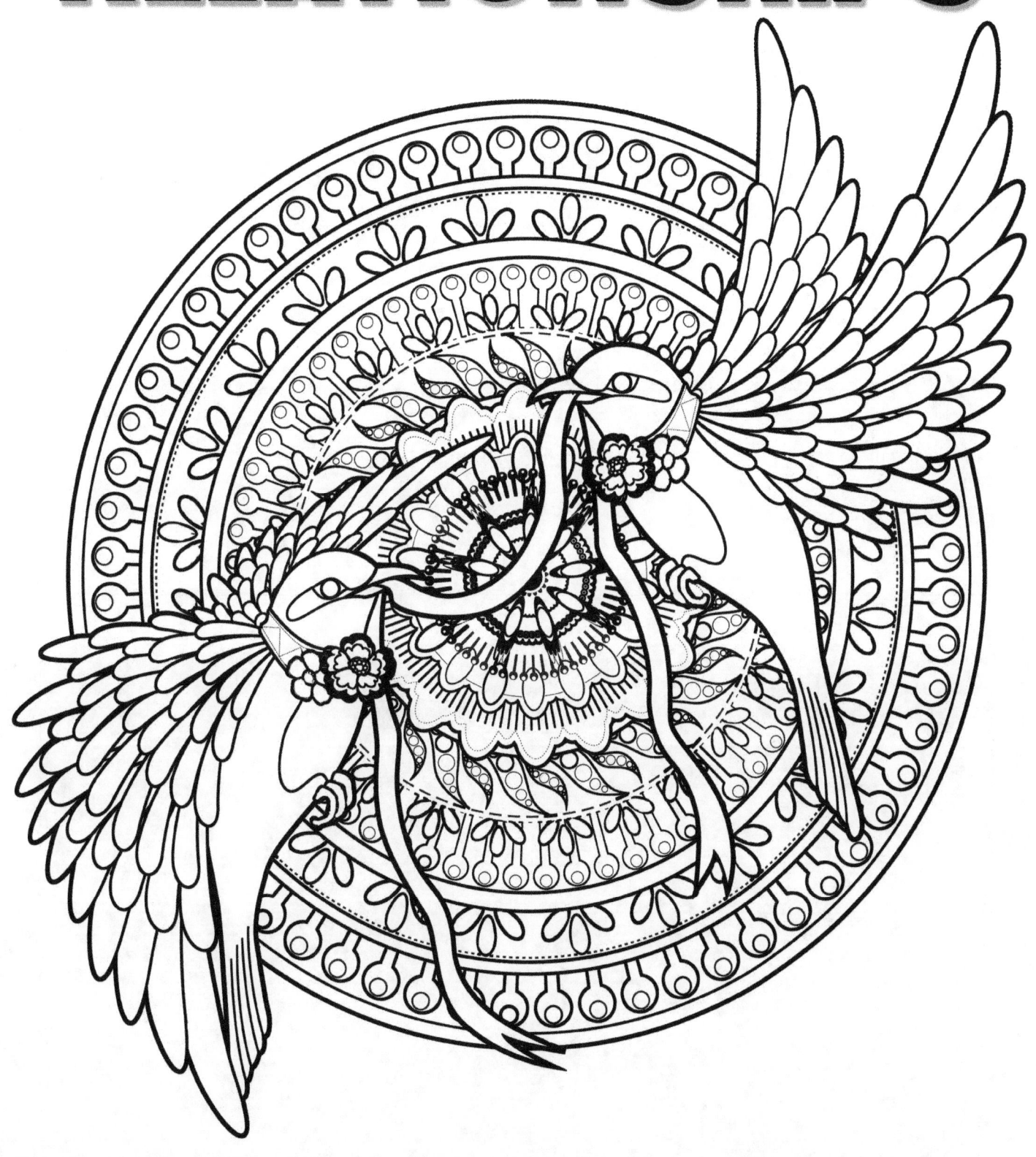

I FOLLOW MY BLISS

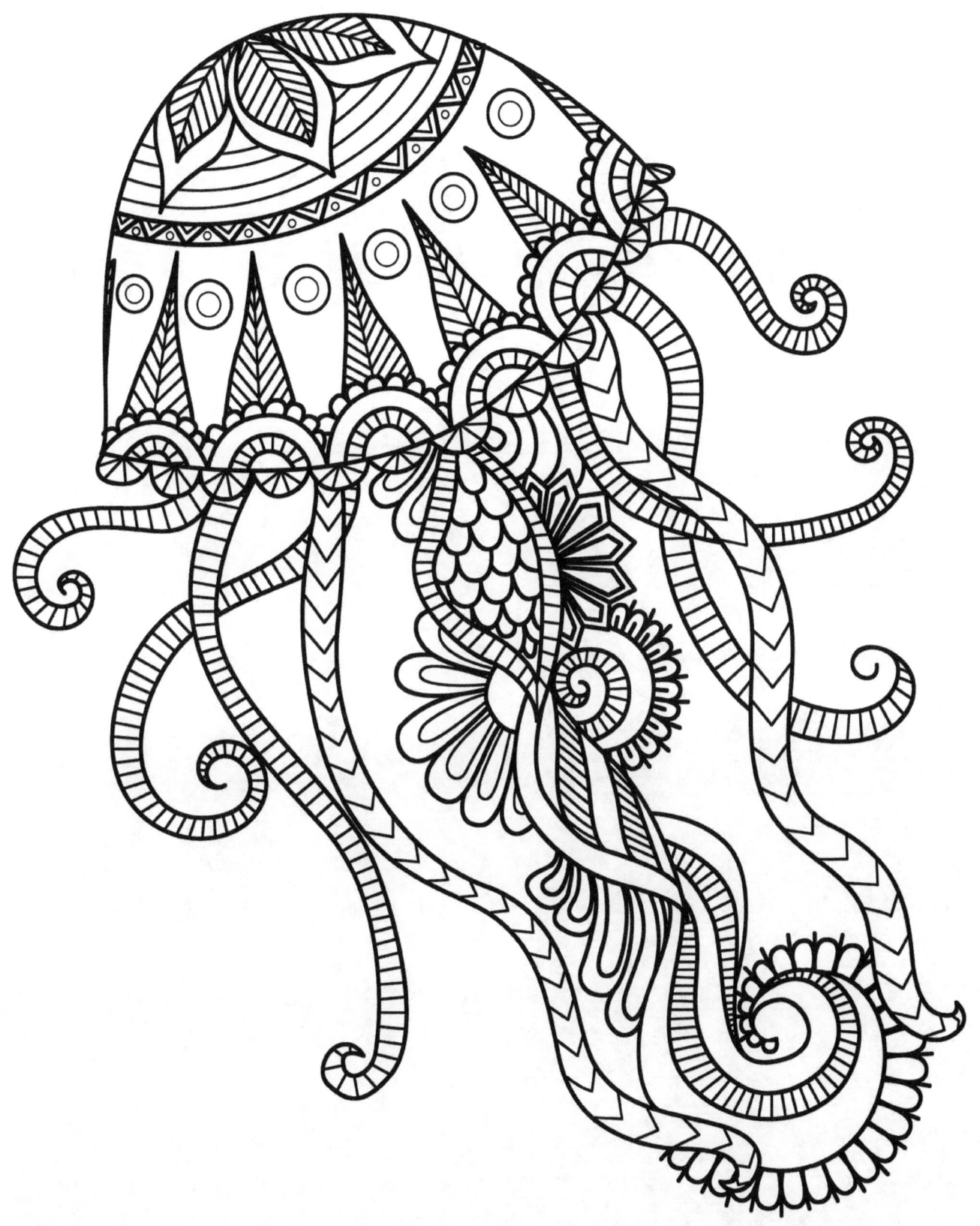

I AM FINDING MY UNKNOWN SPLENDOR

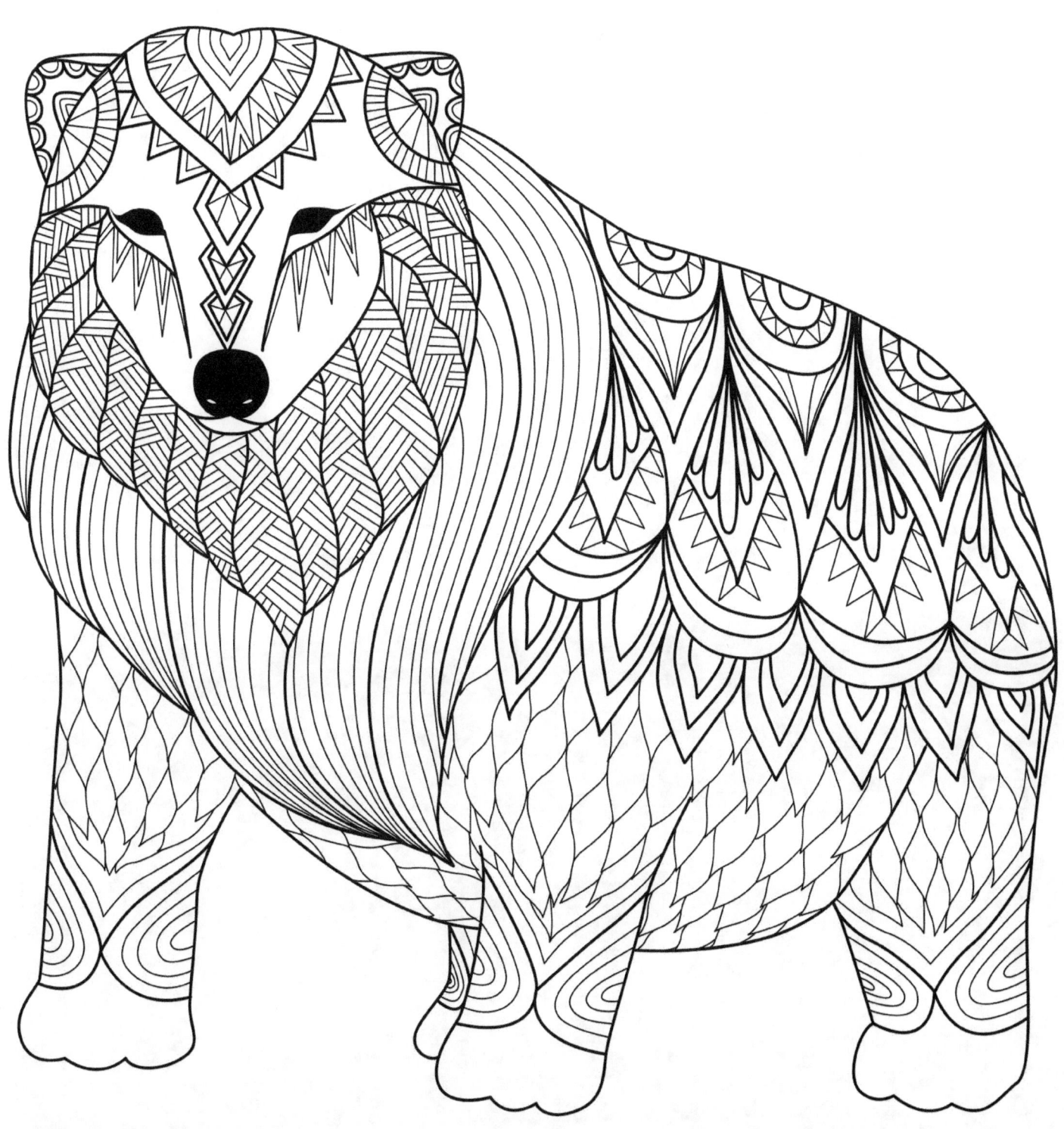

I LOVE BEING ME

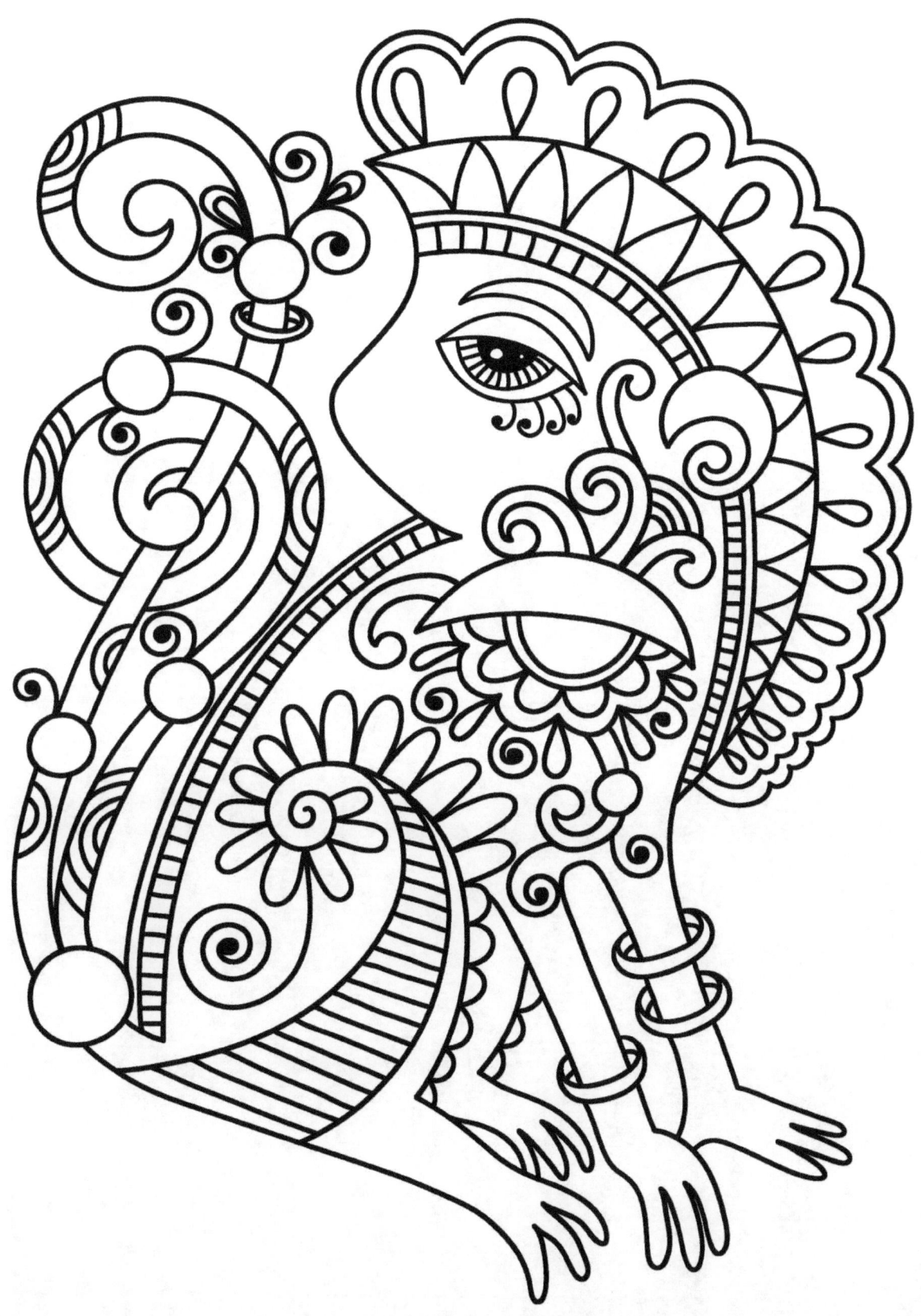

I SEE CHALLENGE AS A BLESSING

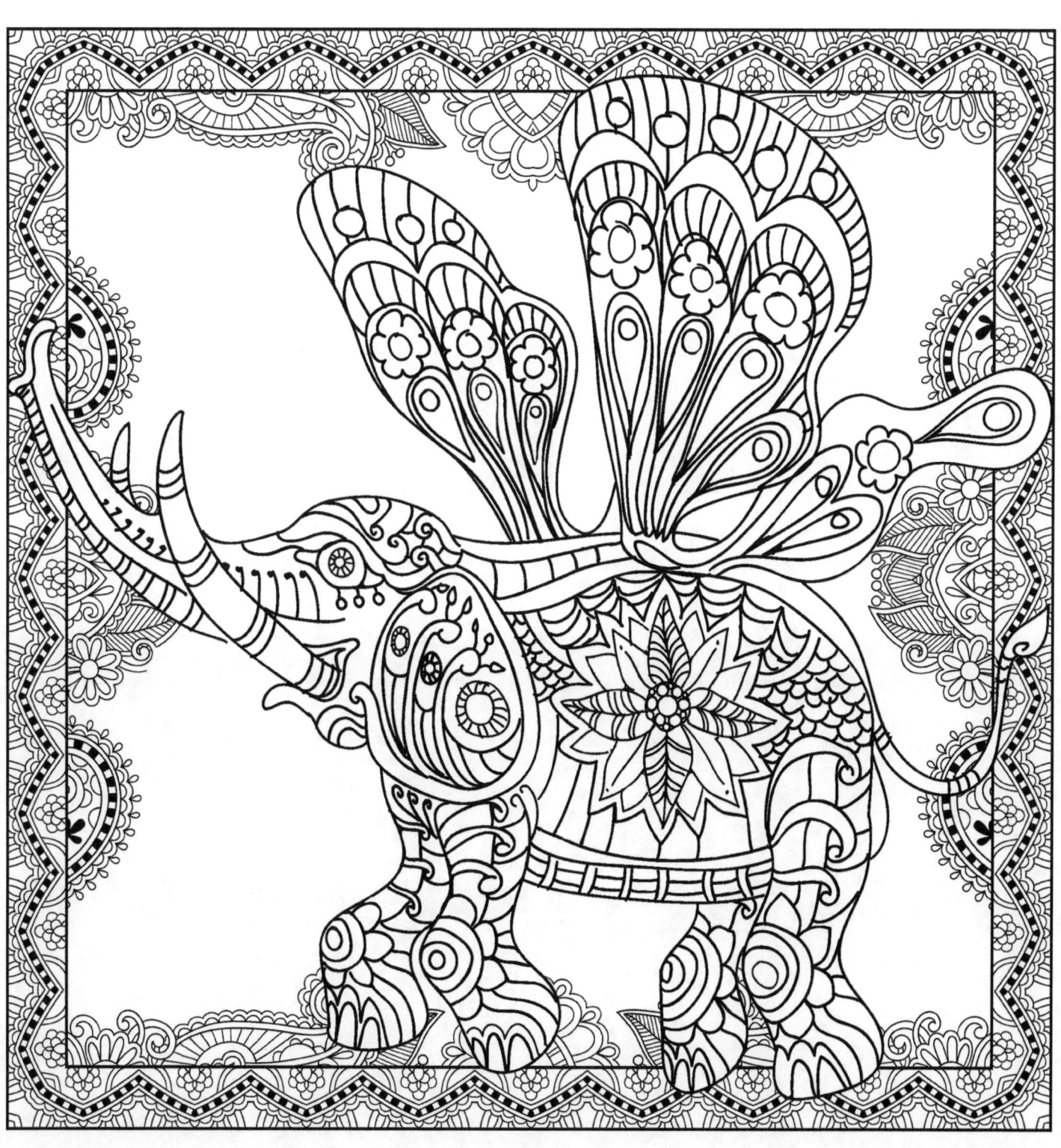

I AM TALENTED

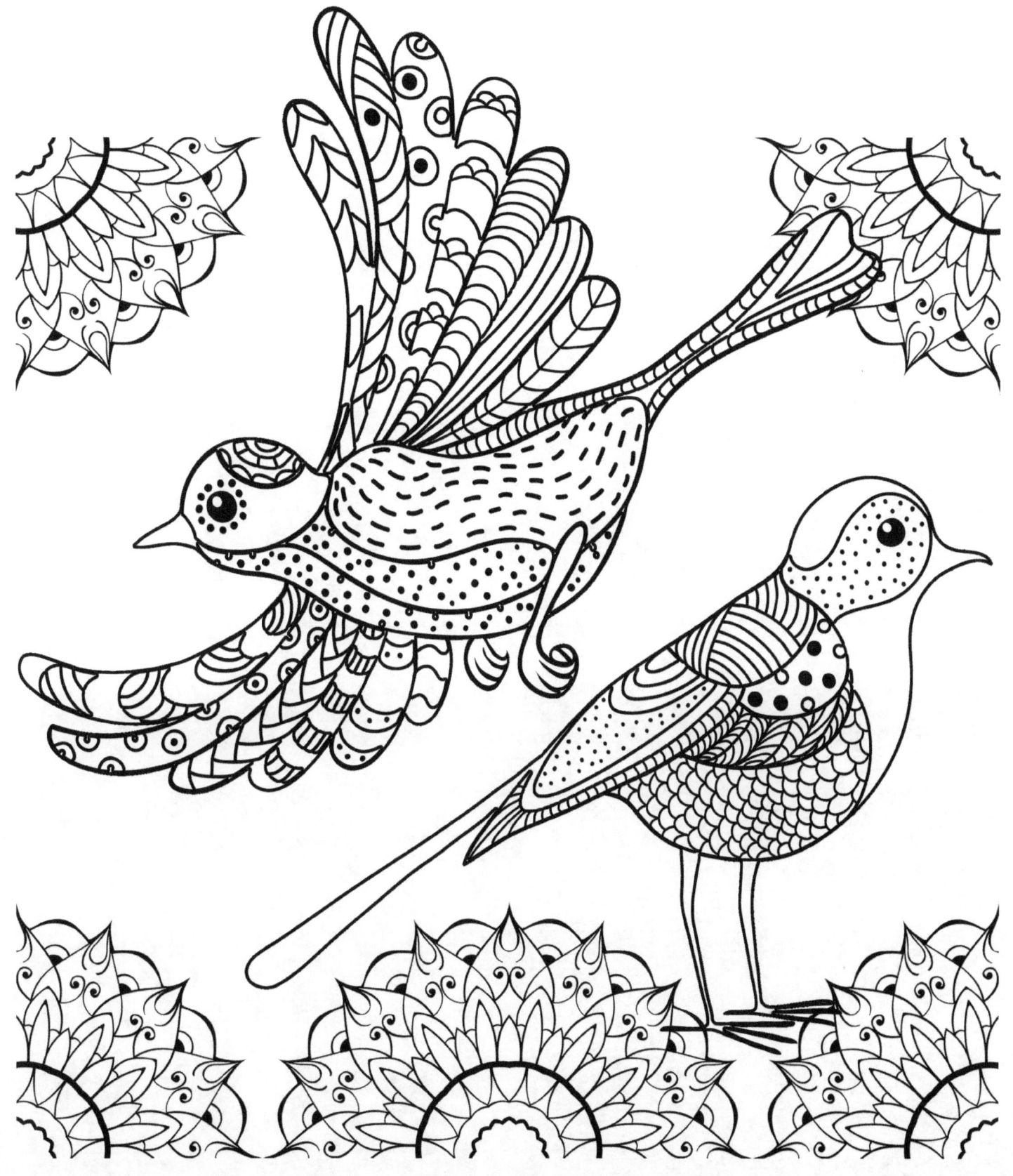

I LIKE MY CHOICES

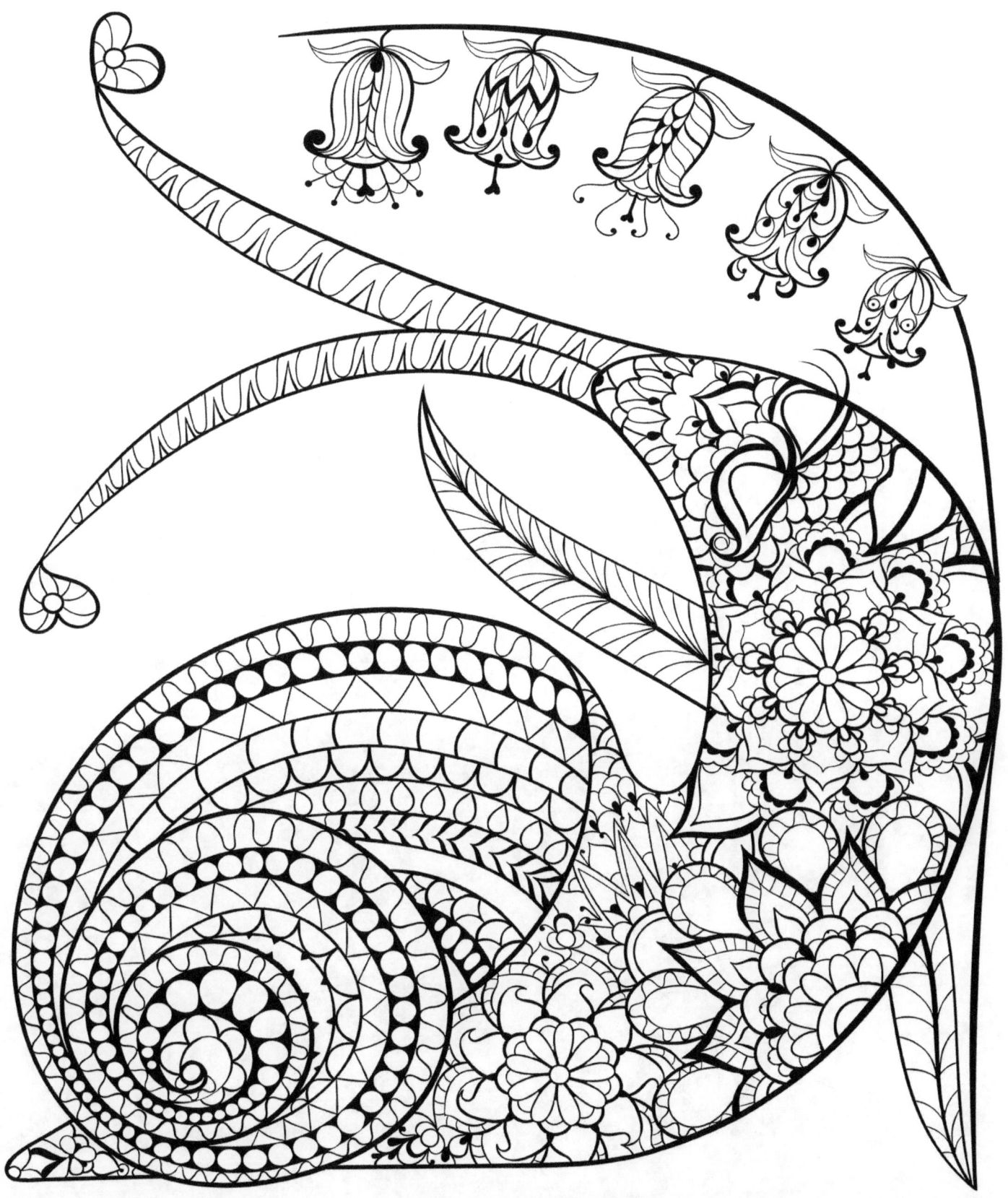

I RELEASE THE NEGATIVE IN LIFE

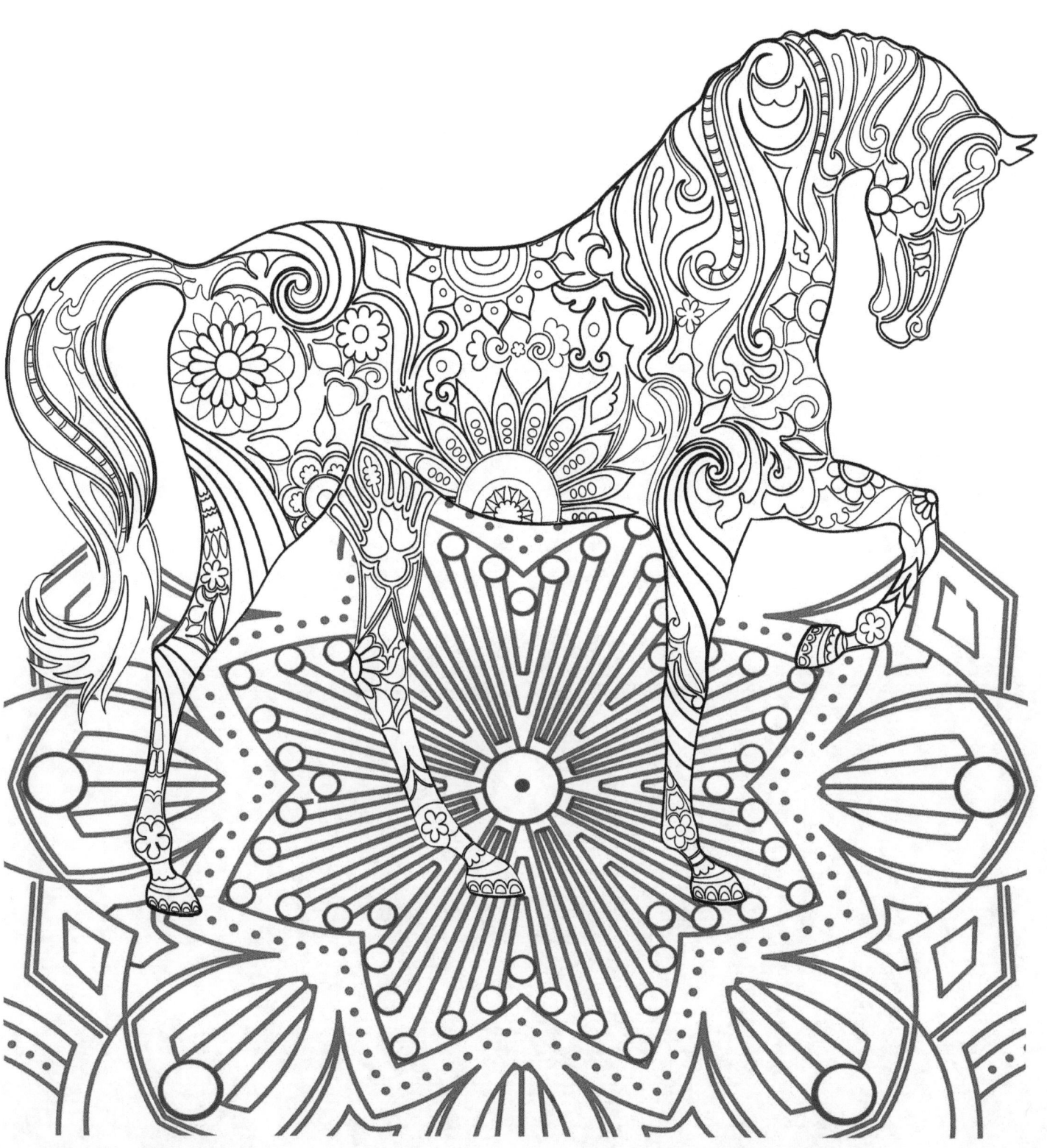

I TRUST MYSELF

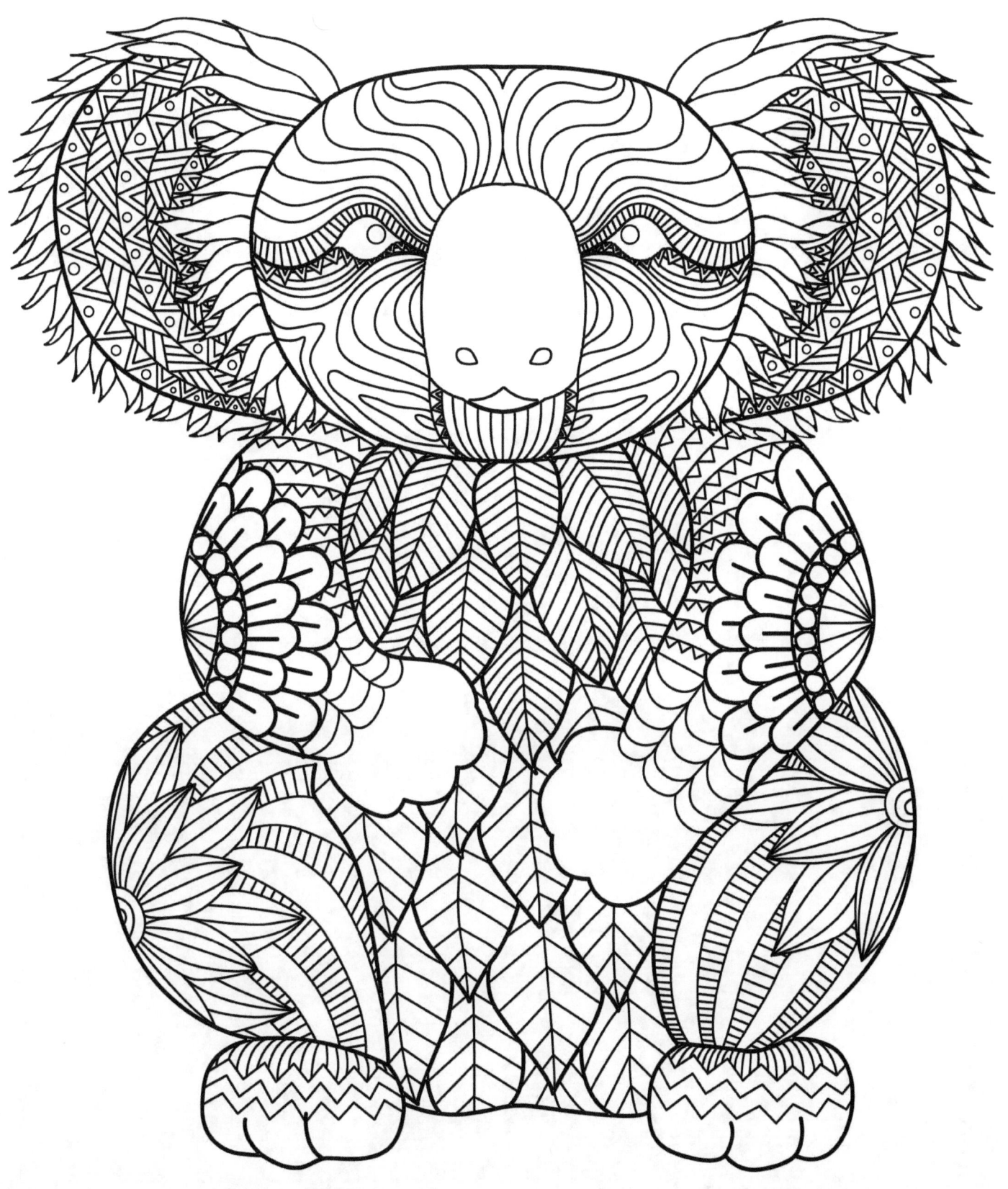

I AM SAFE IN THE WORLD

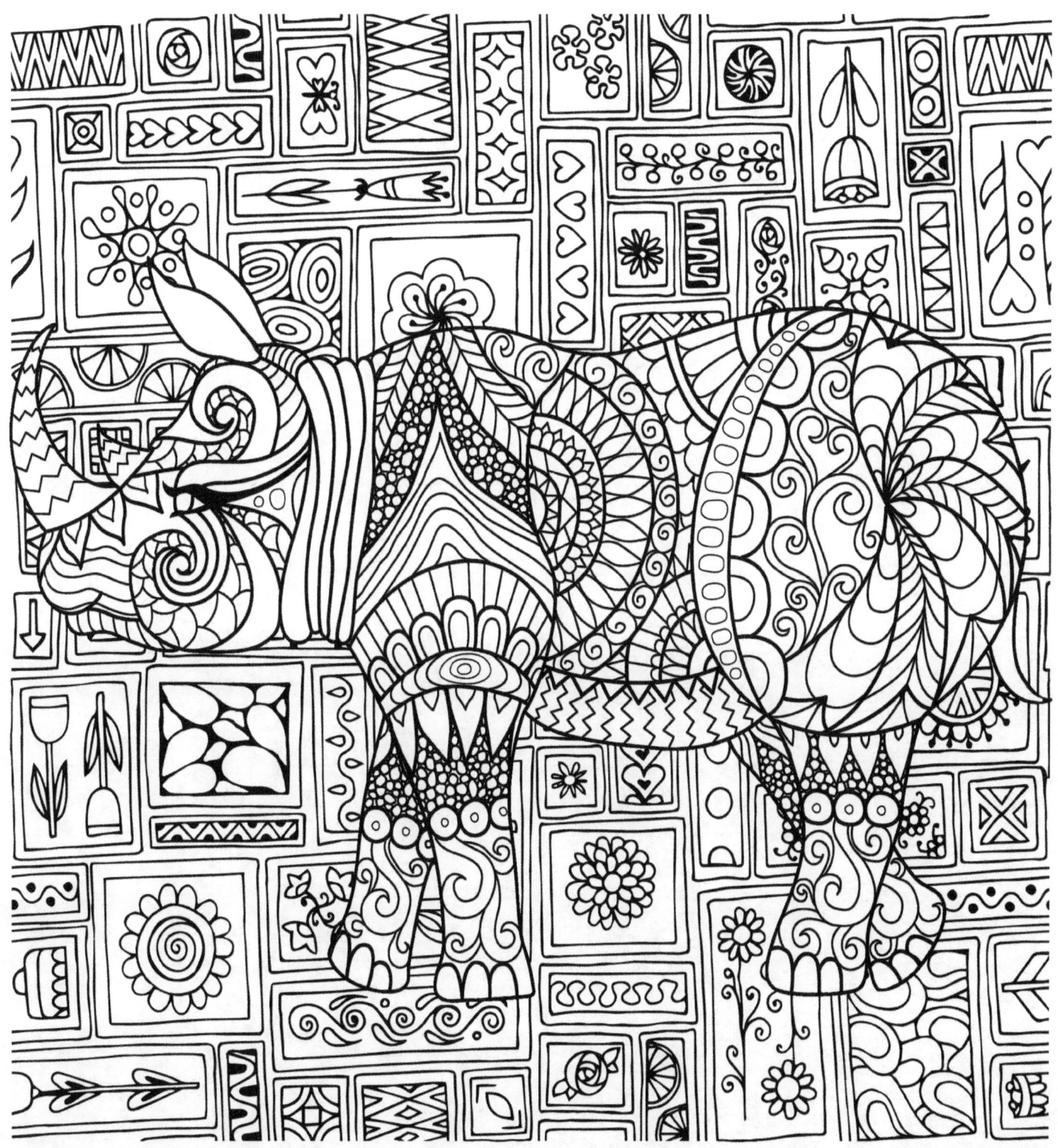

I HAVE PATIENCE

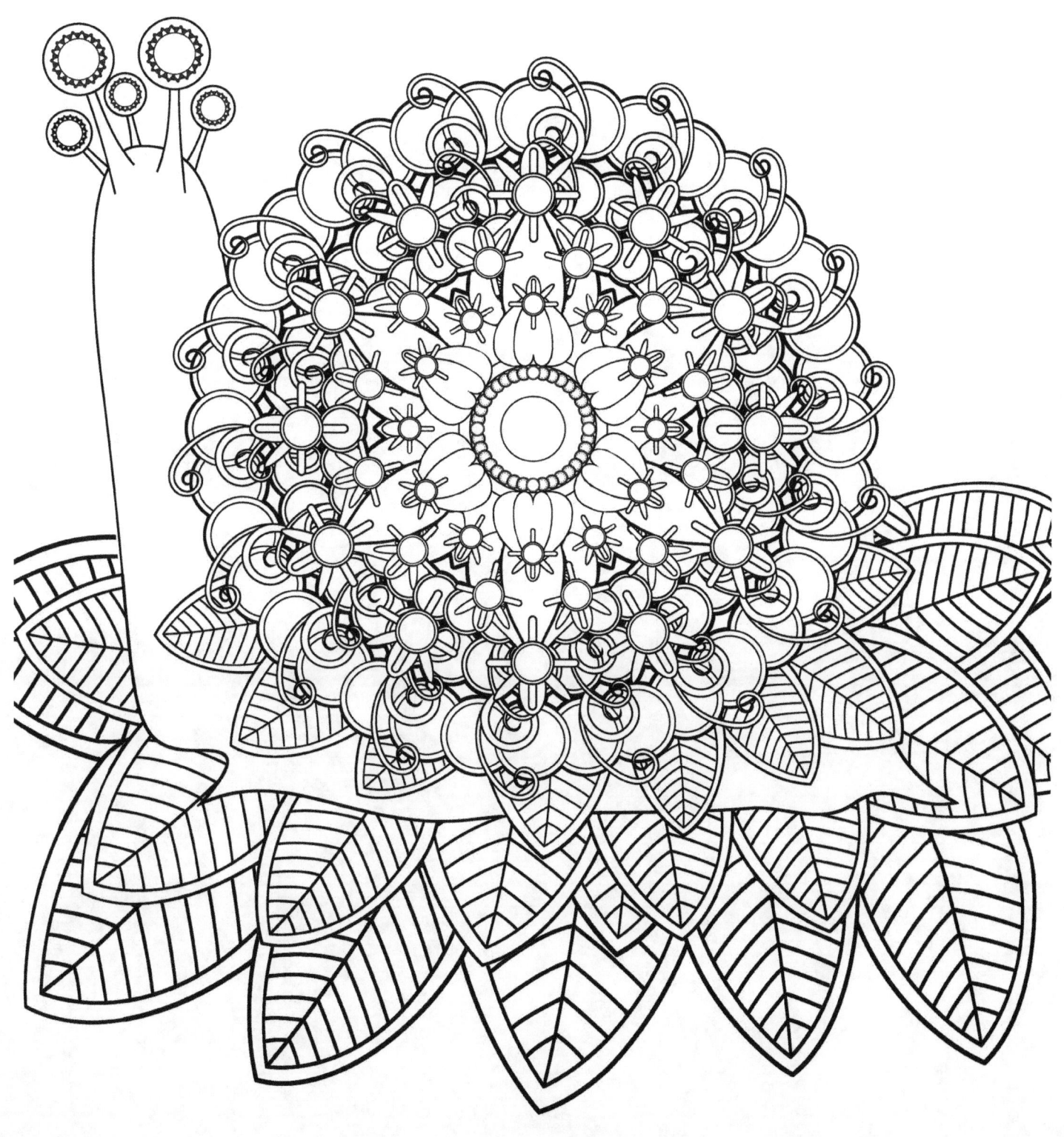

I AM MY OWN BEST FRIEND

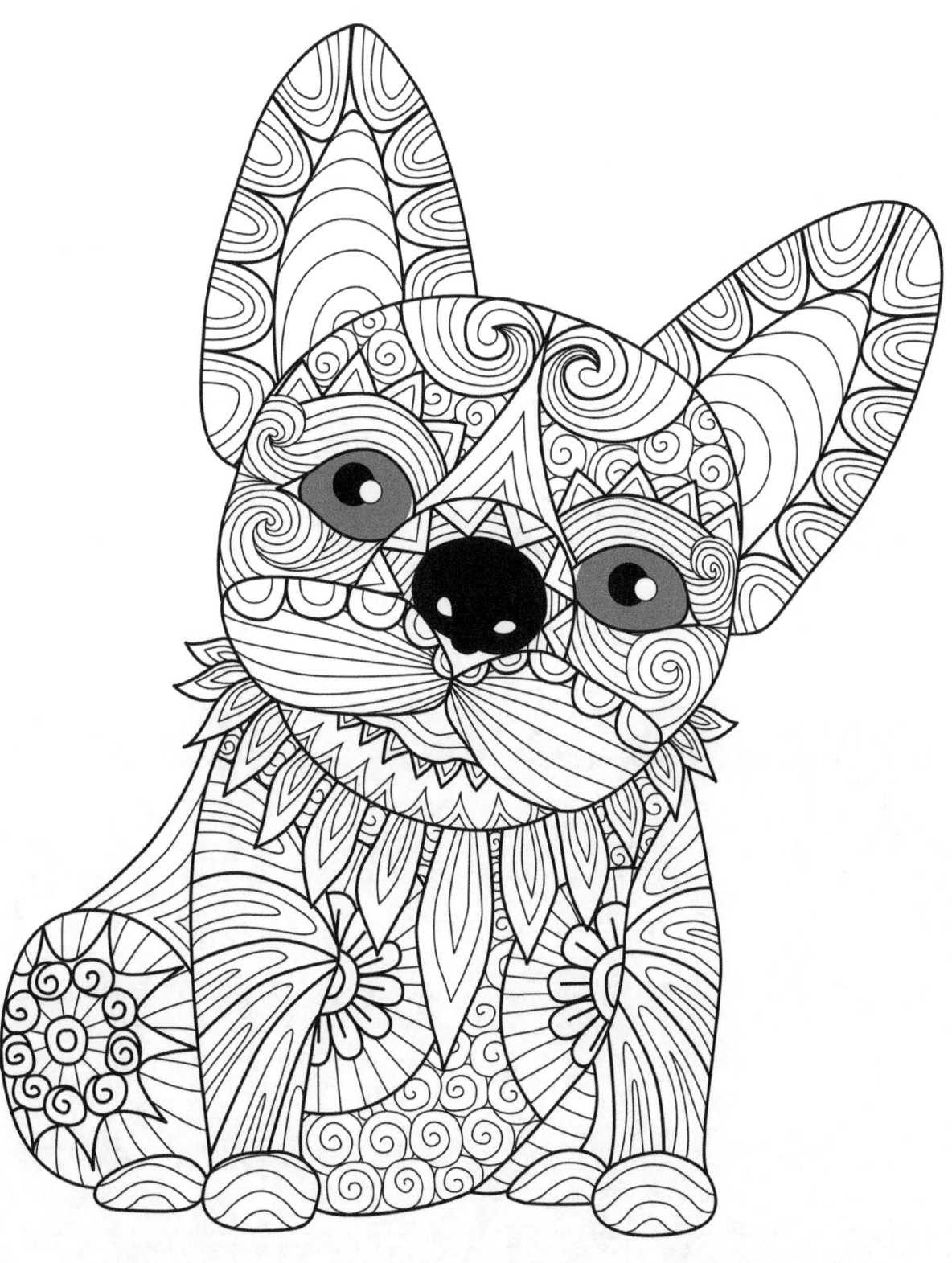

I CAN ALWAYS UPLIFT MYSELF

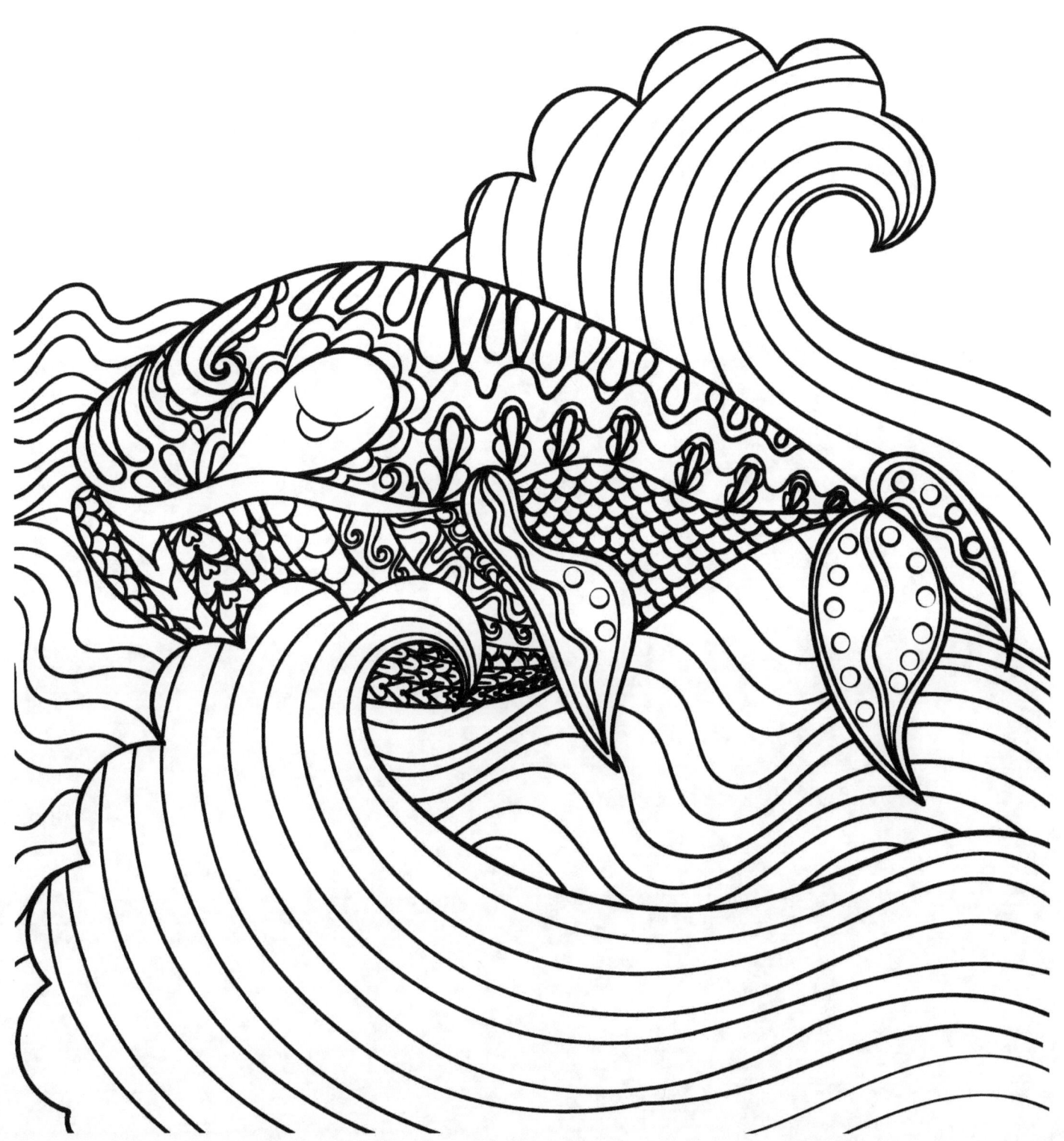

I LOVE MY ESSENCE OF STRENGTH

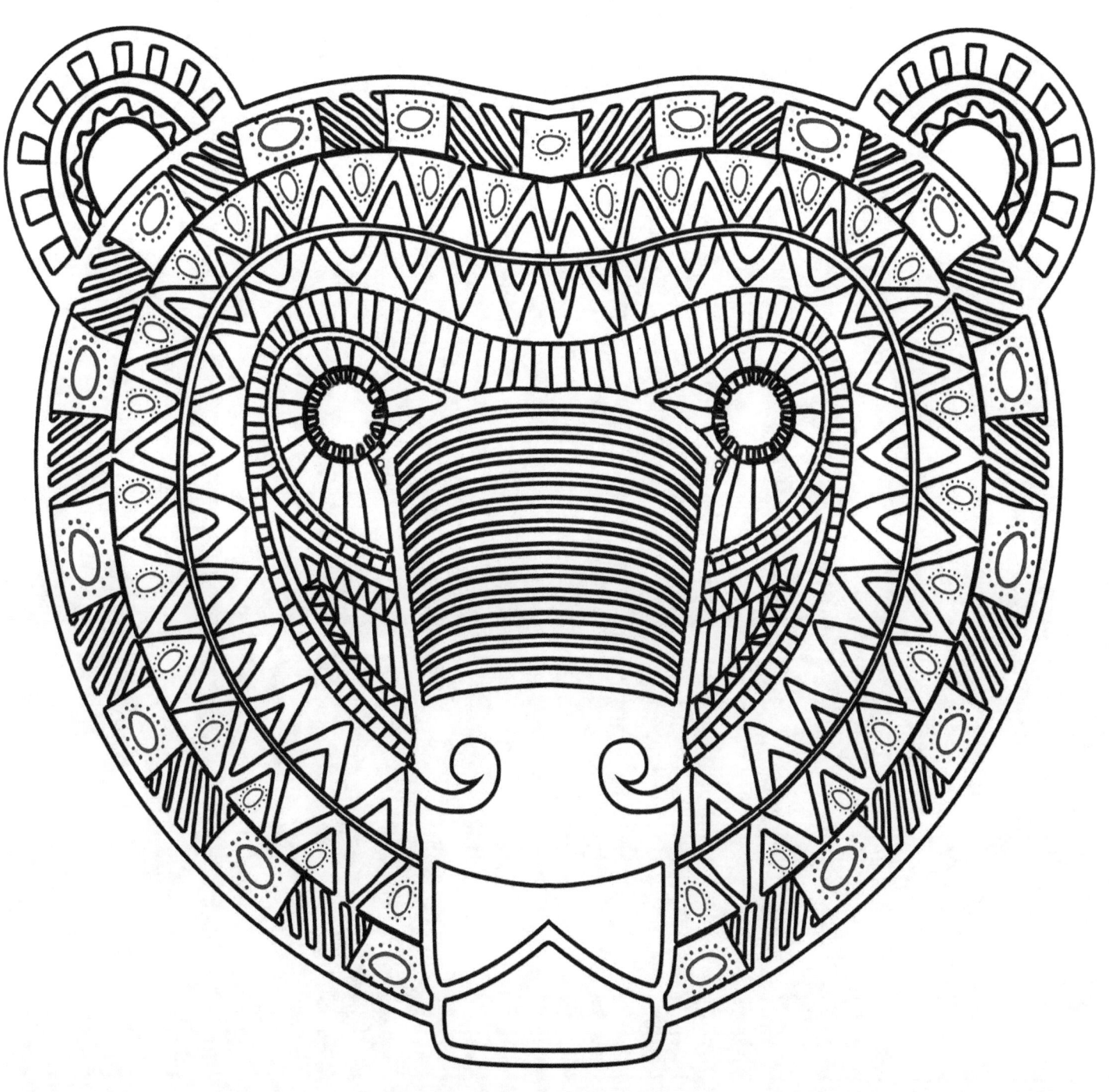

I AM GOOD AT FINDING SOLUTIONS

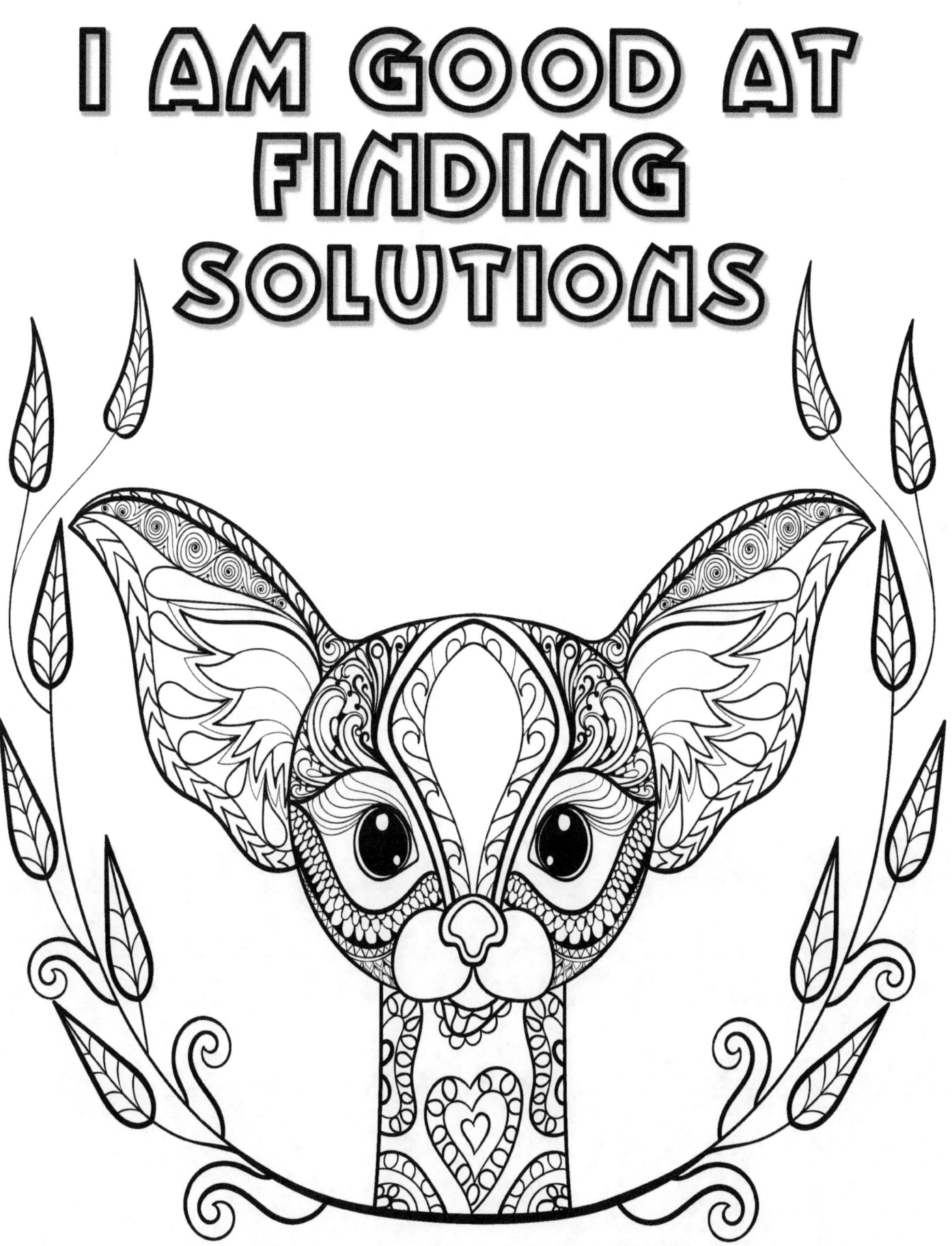

I THINK OUTSIDE THE BOX

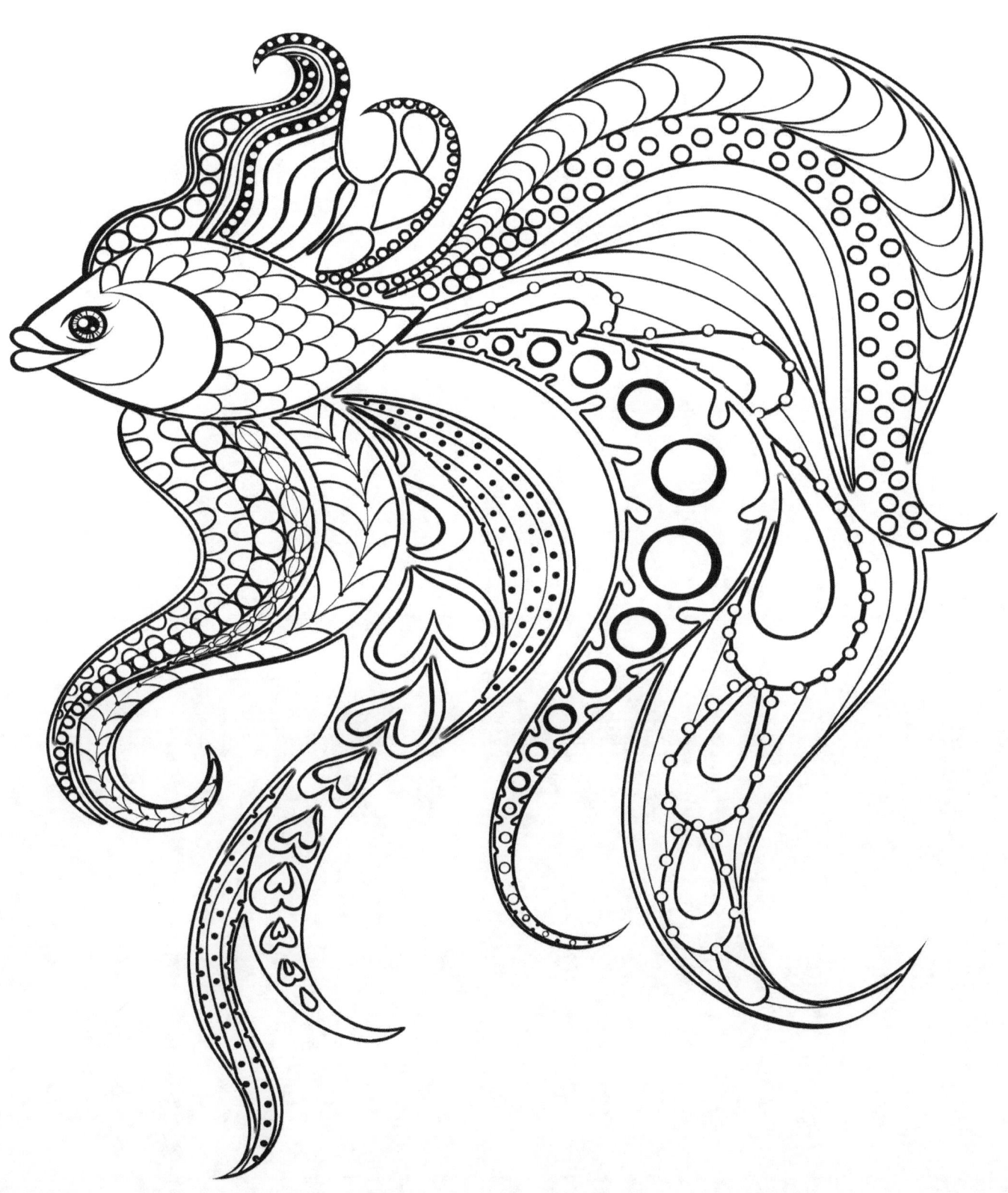

I AM RESPECTED

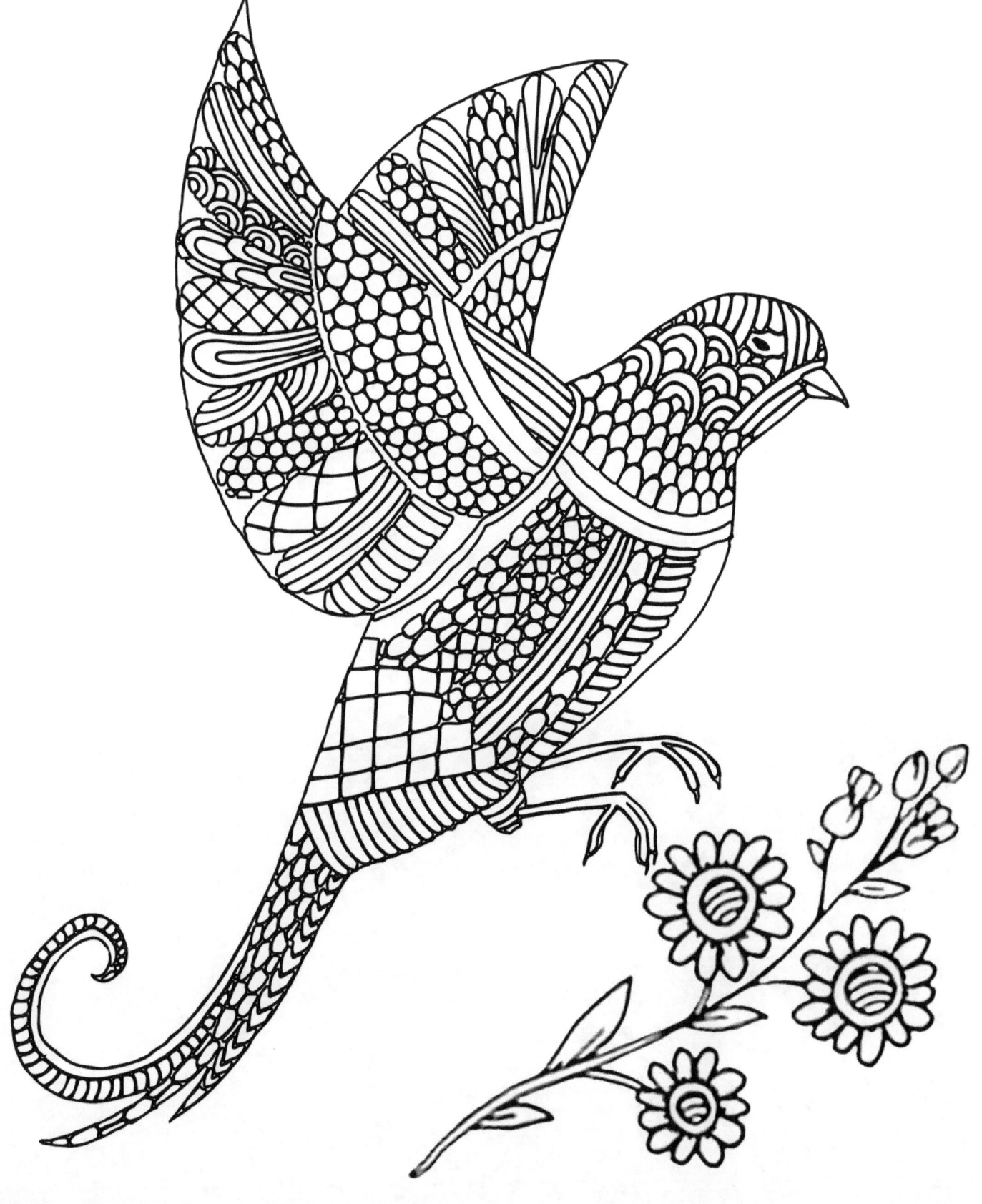

I BELIEVE IN MYSELF

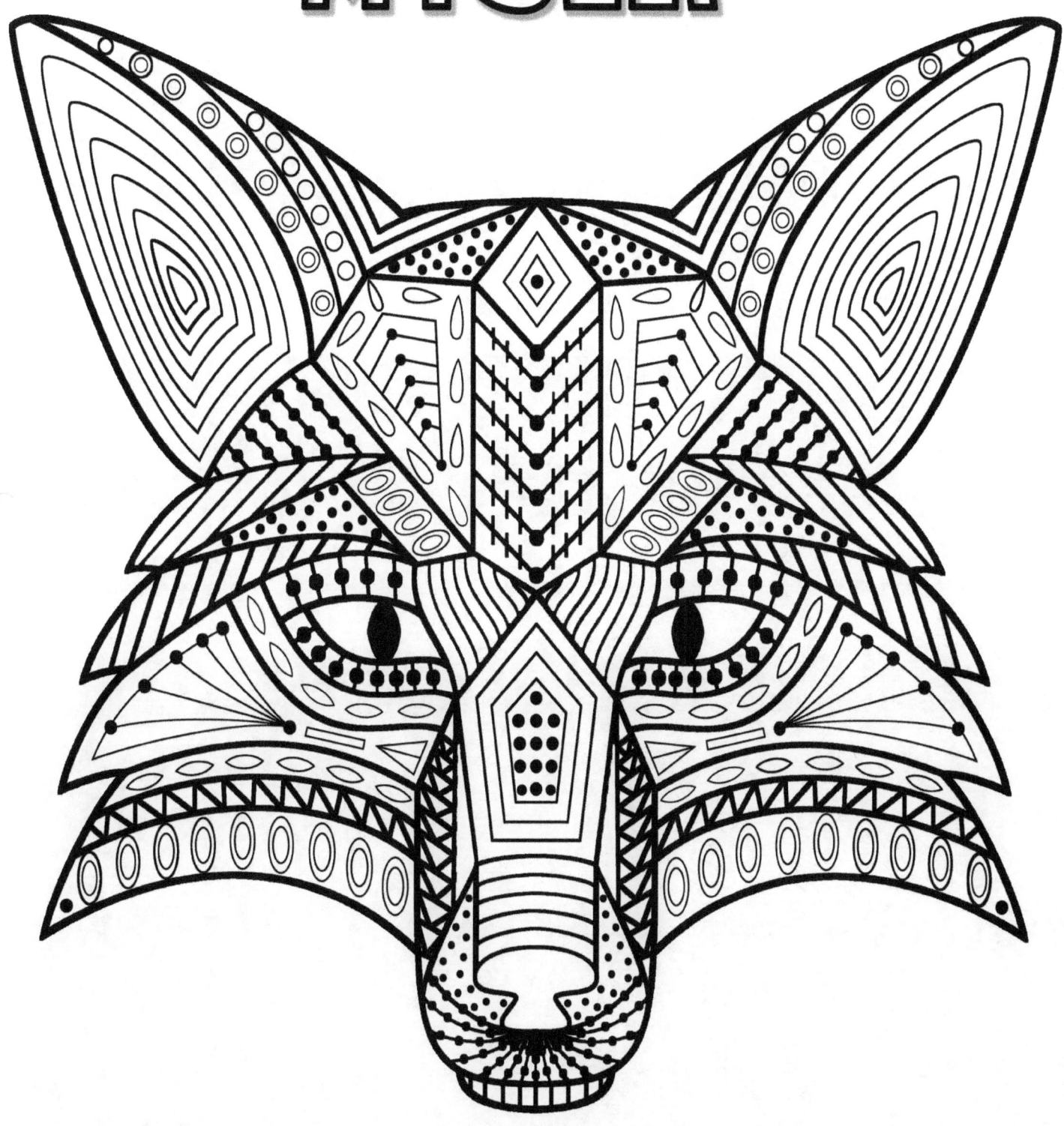

I SEE OTHERS AS PRECIOUS

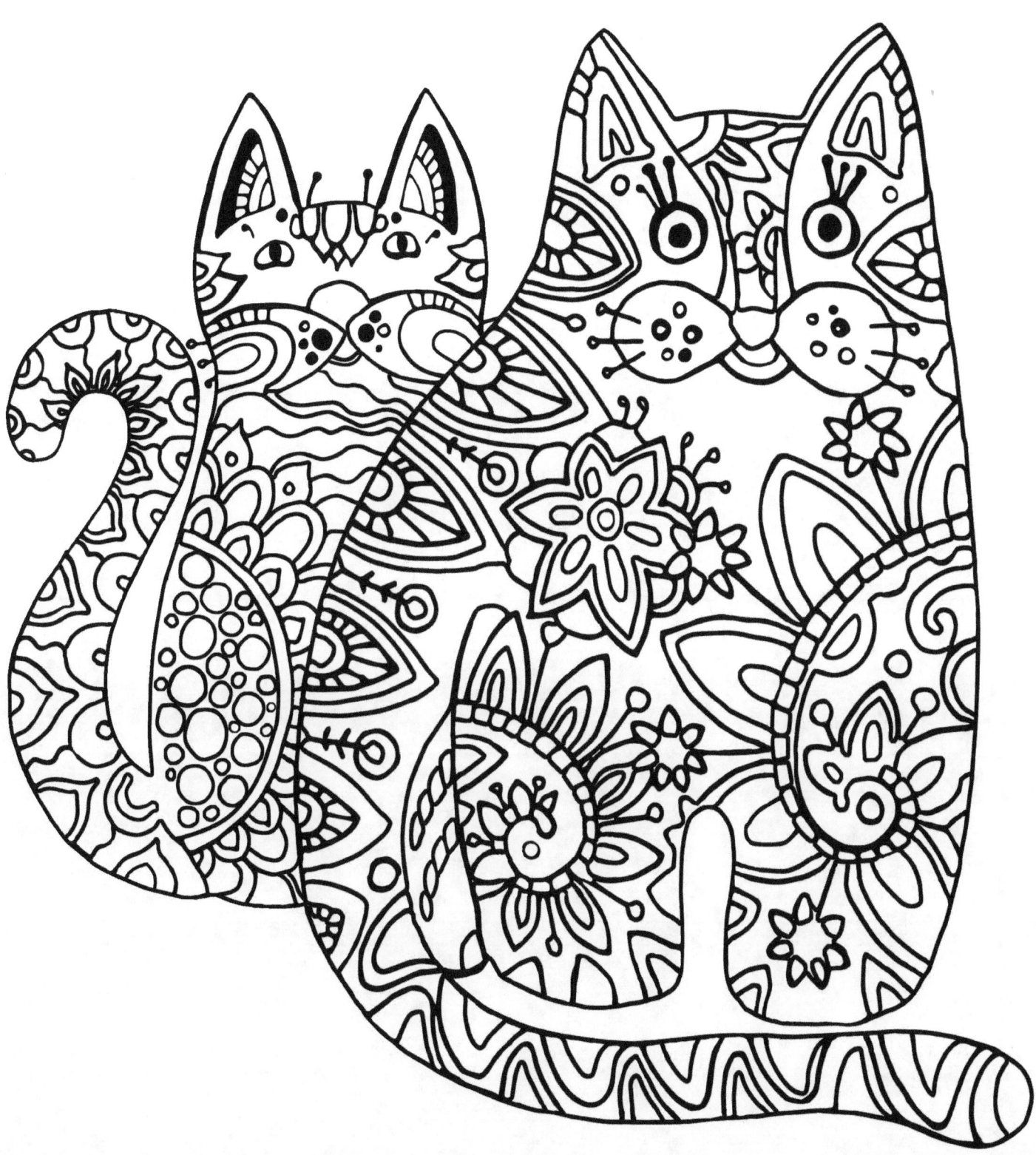

MY HEART AND MY MIND ARE OPEN

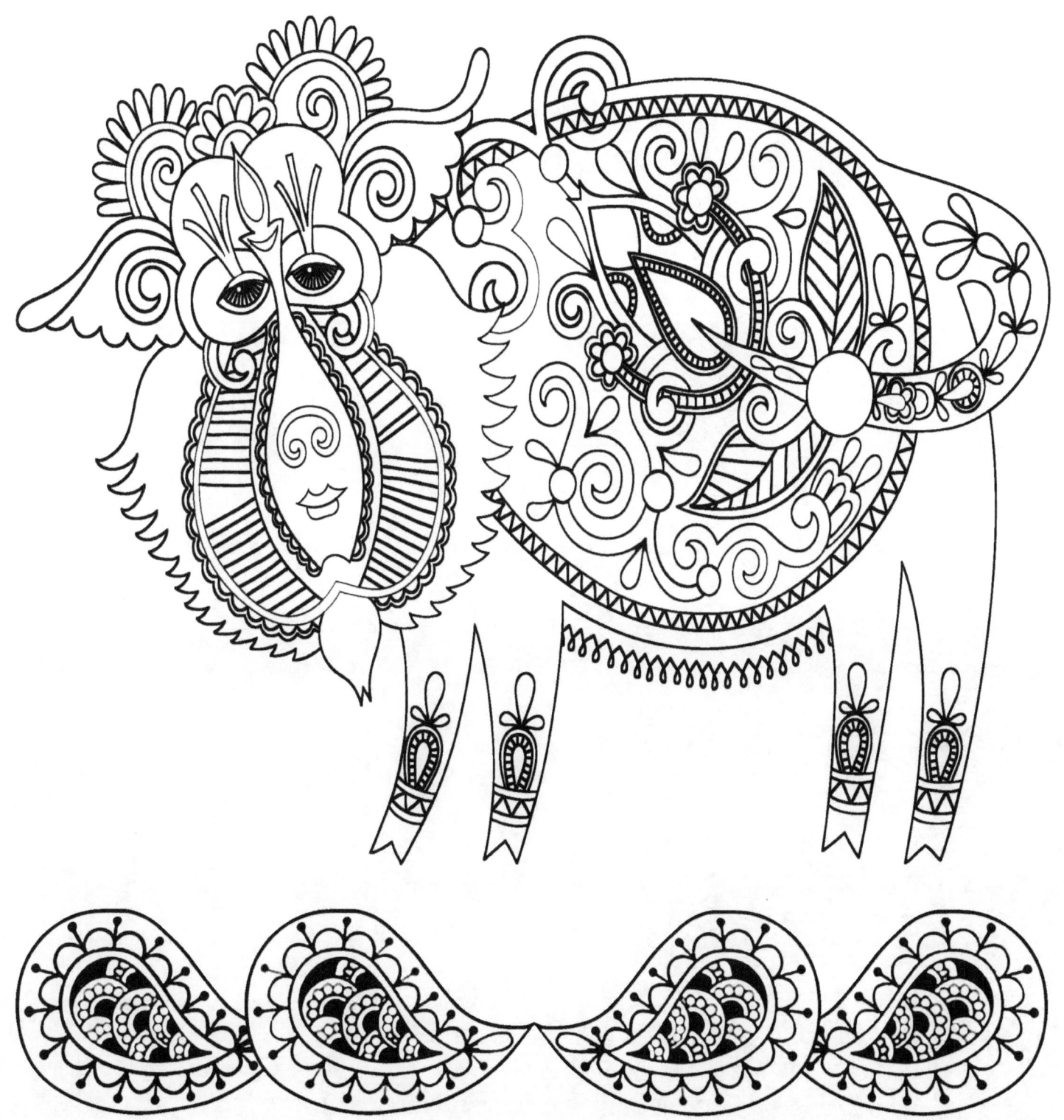

I FEEL ALIVE

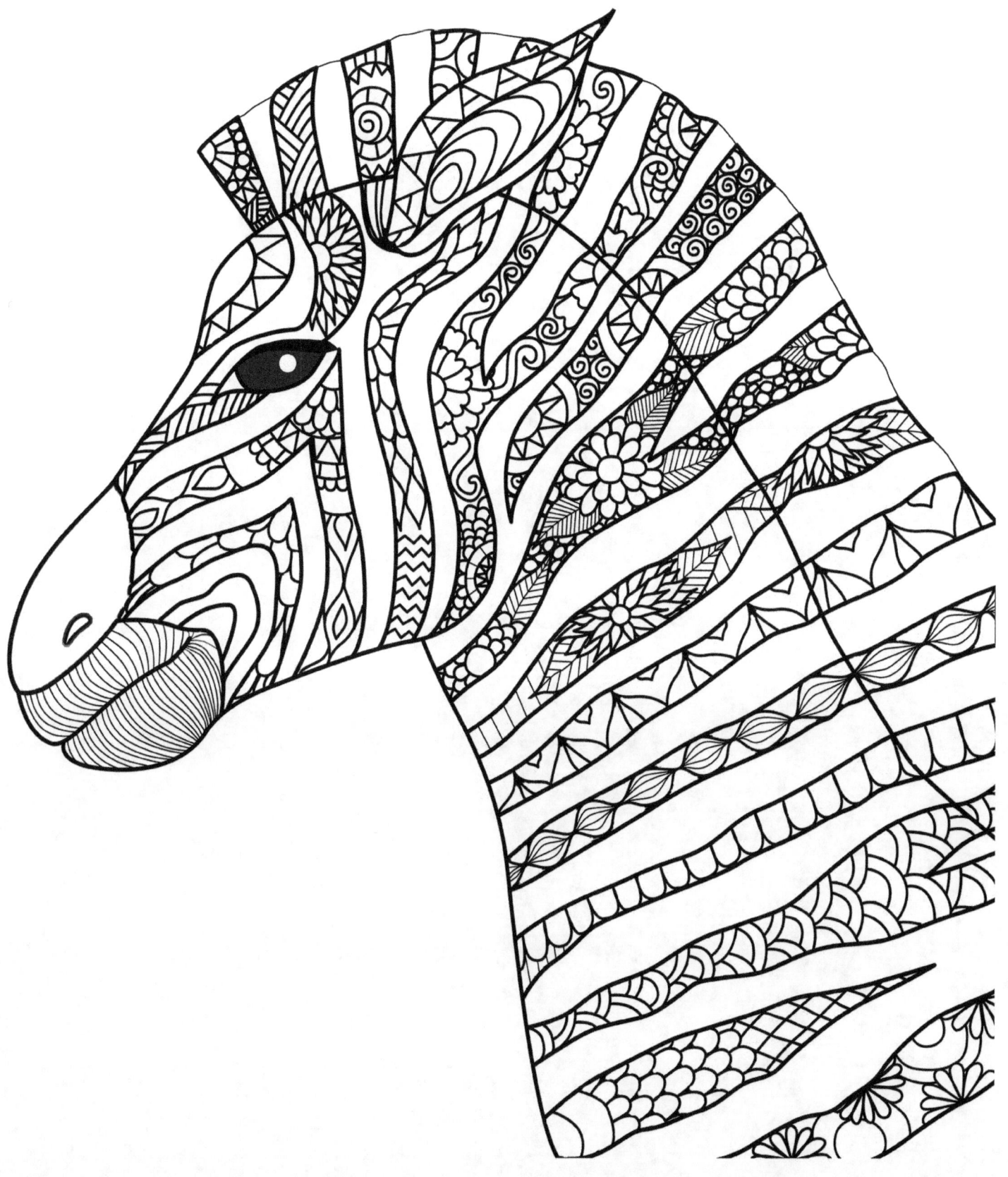

I CAN AFFORD TO BE GENEROUS

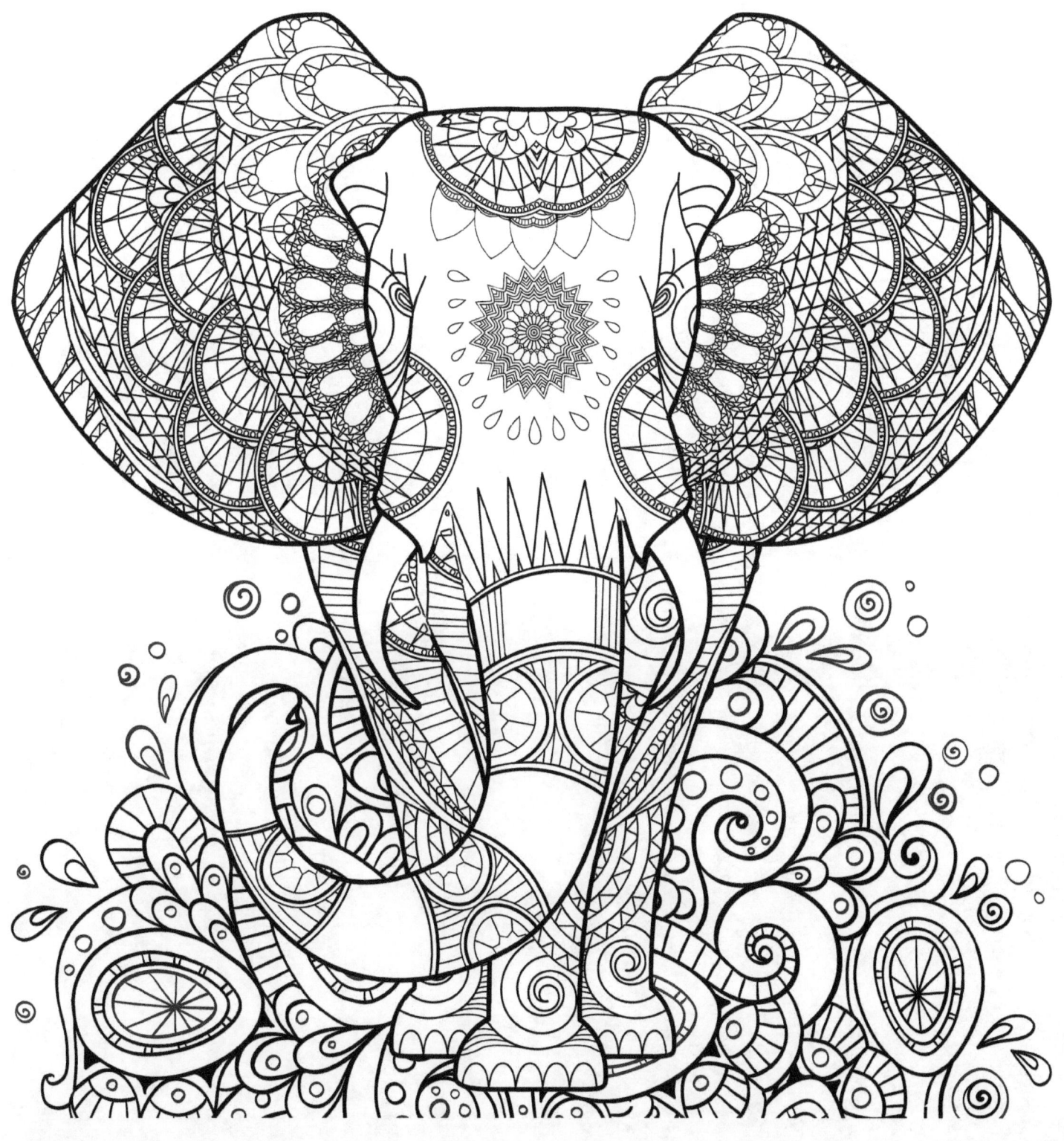

I AM AMONG FRIENDS EVERYWHERE

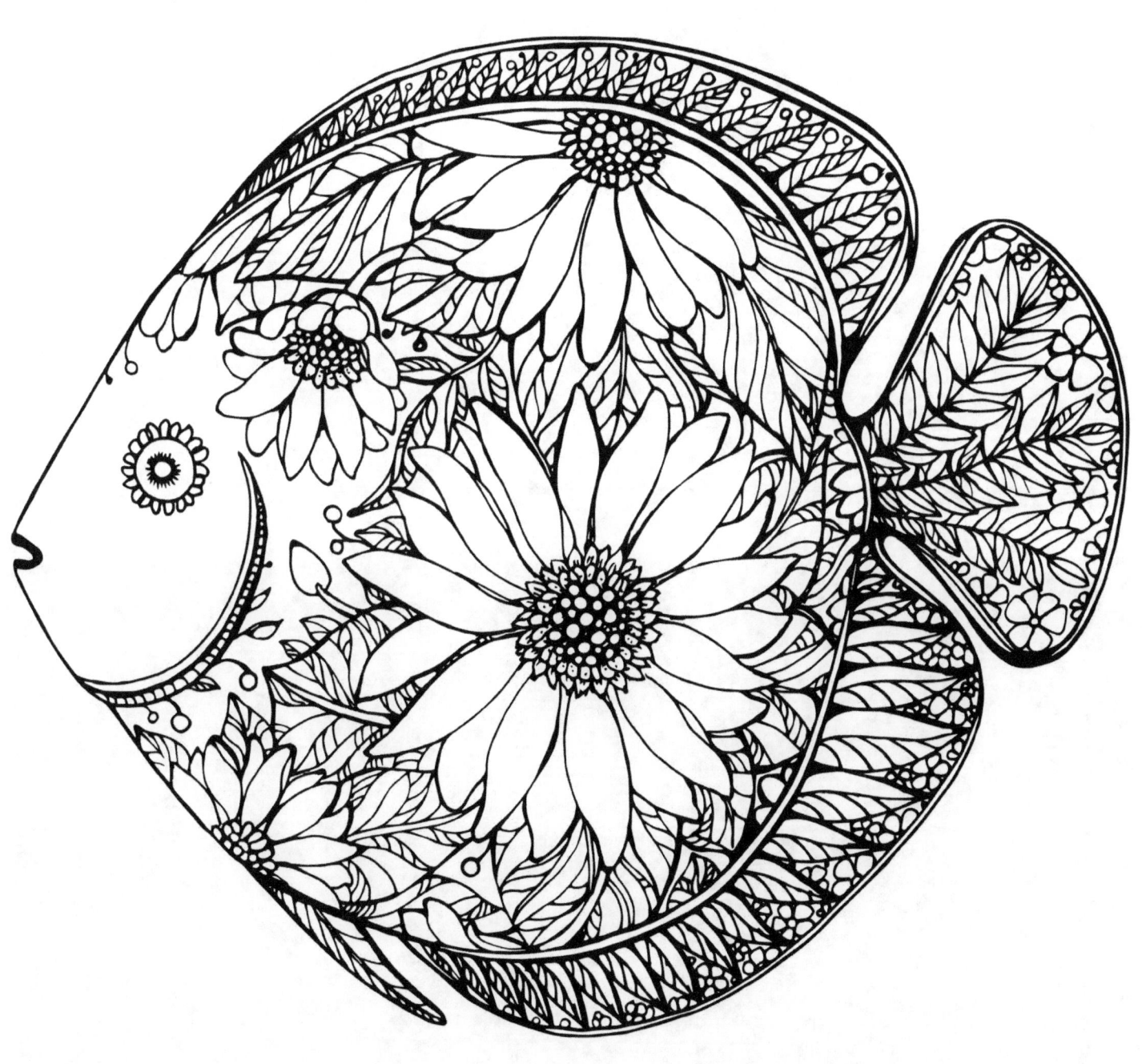

I FOLLOW MY INNER GUIDANCE

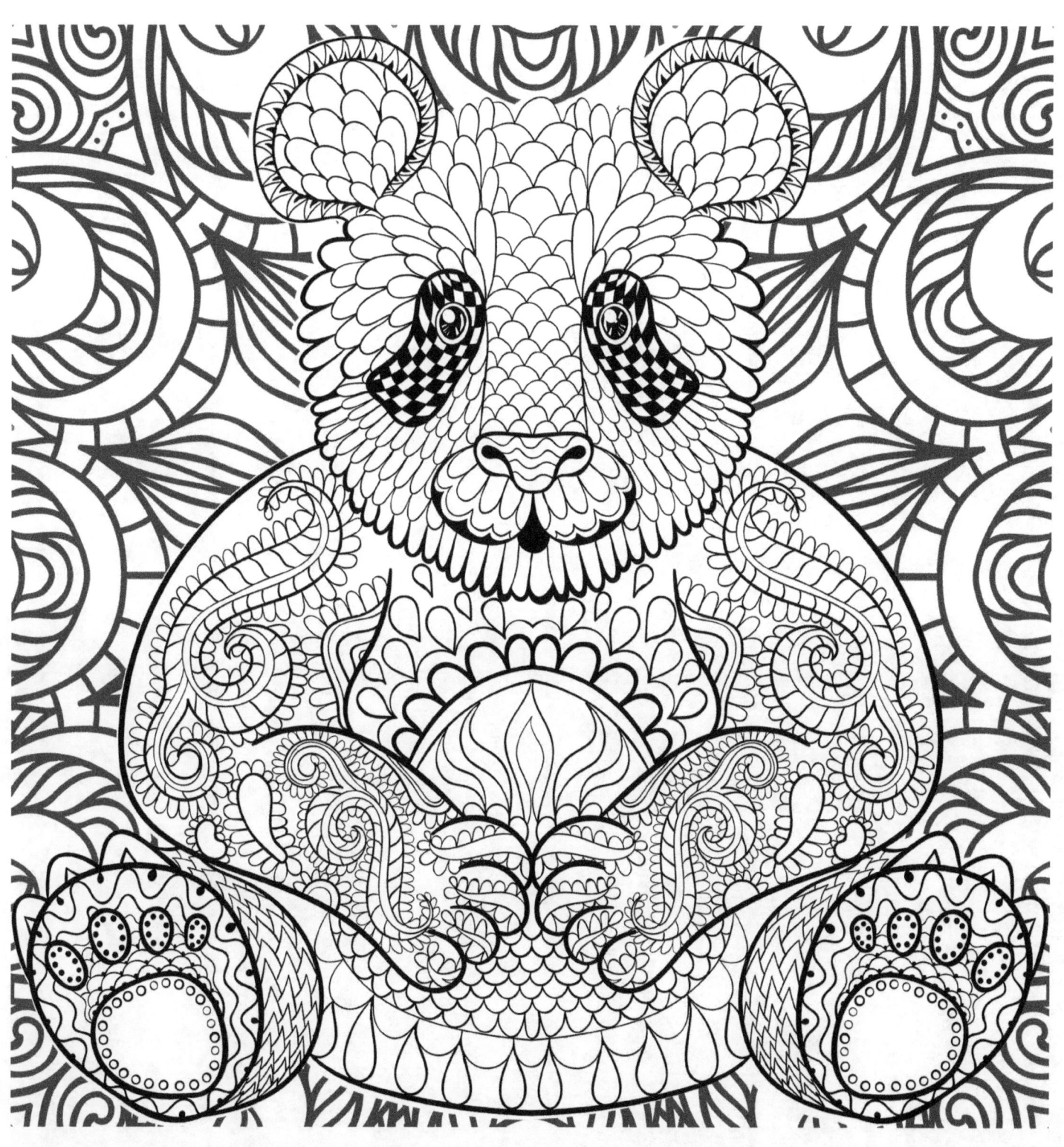

I AM OPEN TO PLEASURE

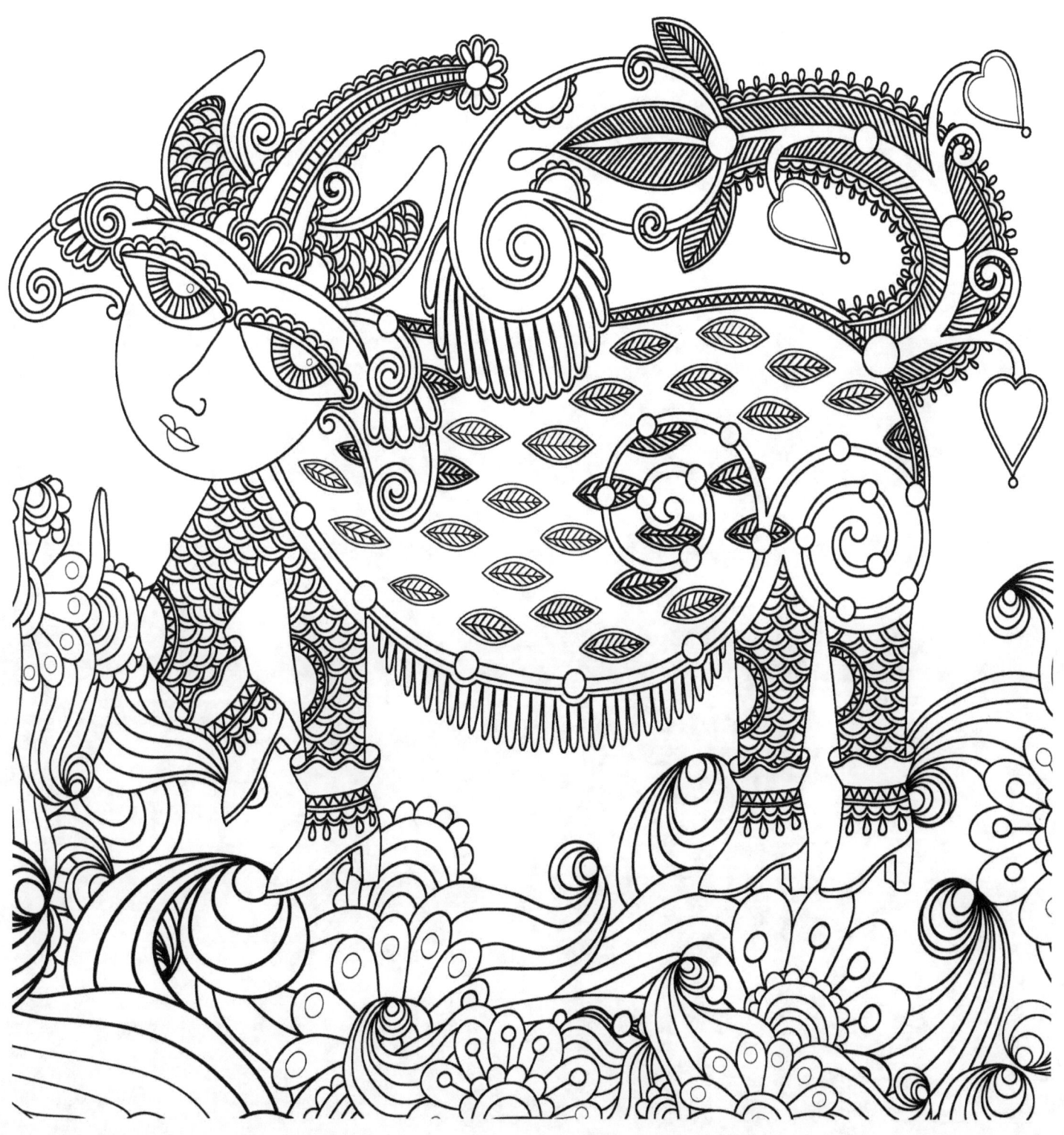

I TAKE THE LEAP OF LIFE

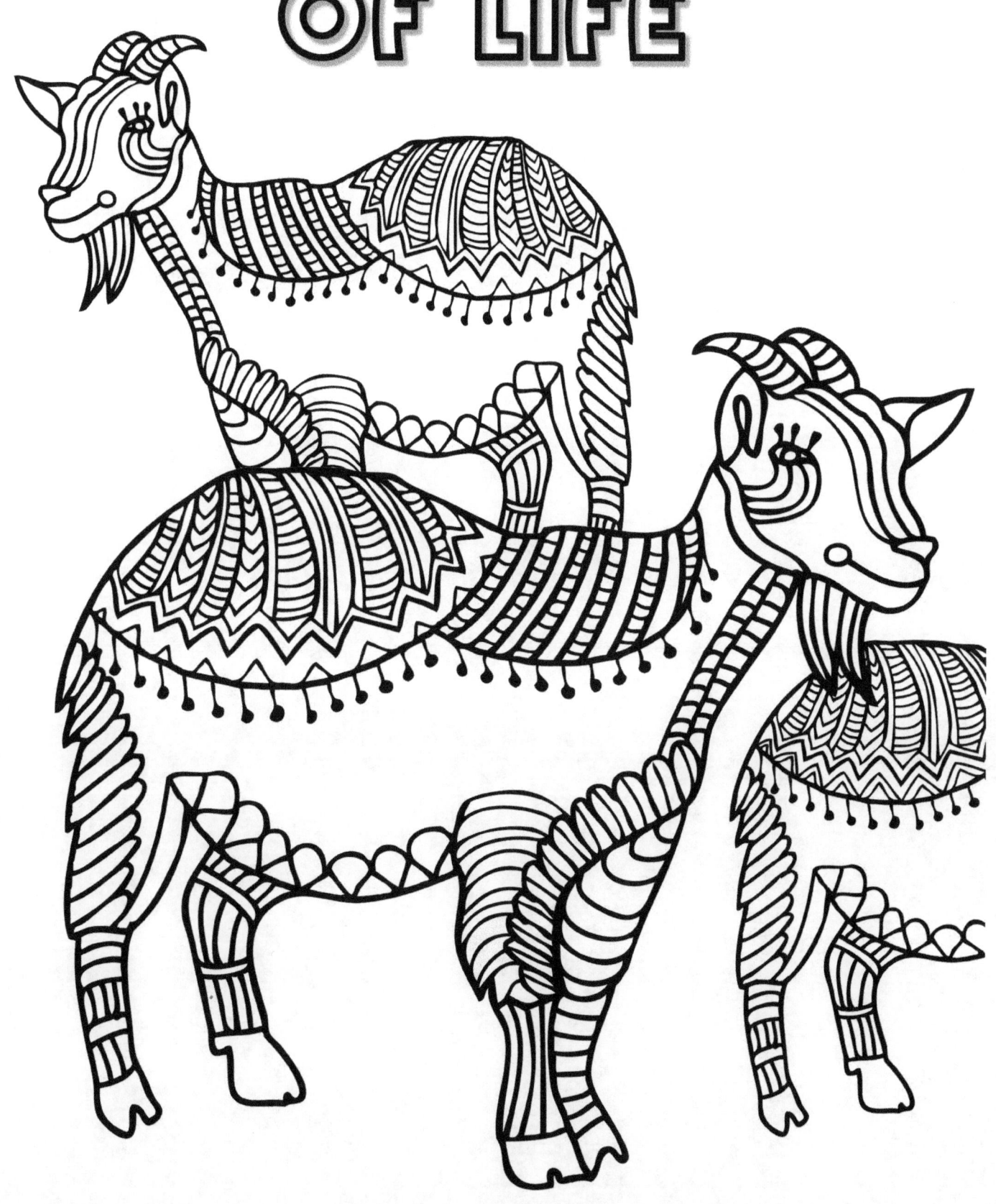

WHAT I AM IS WHAT I AM

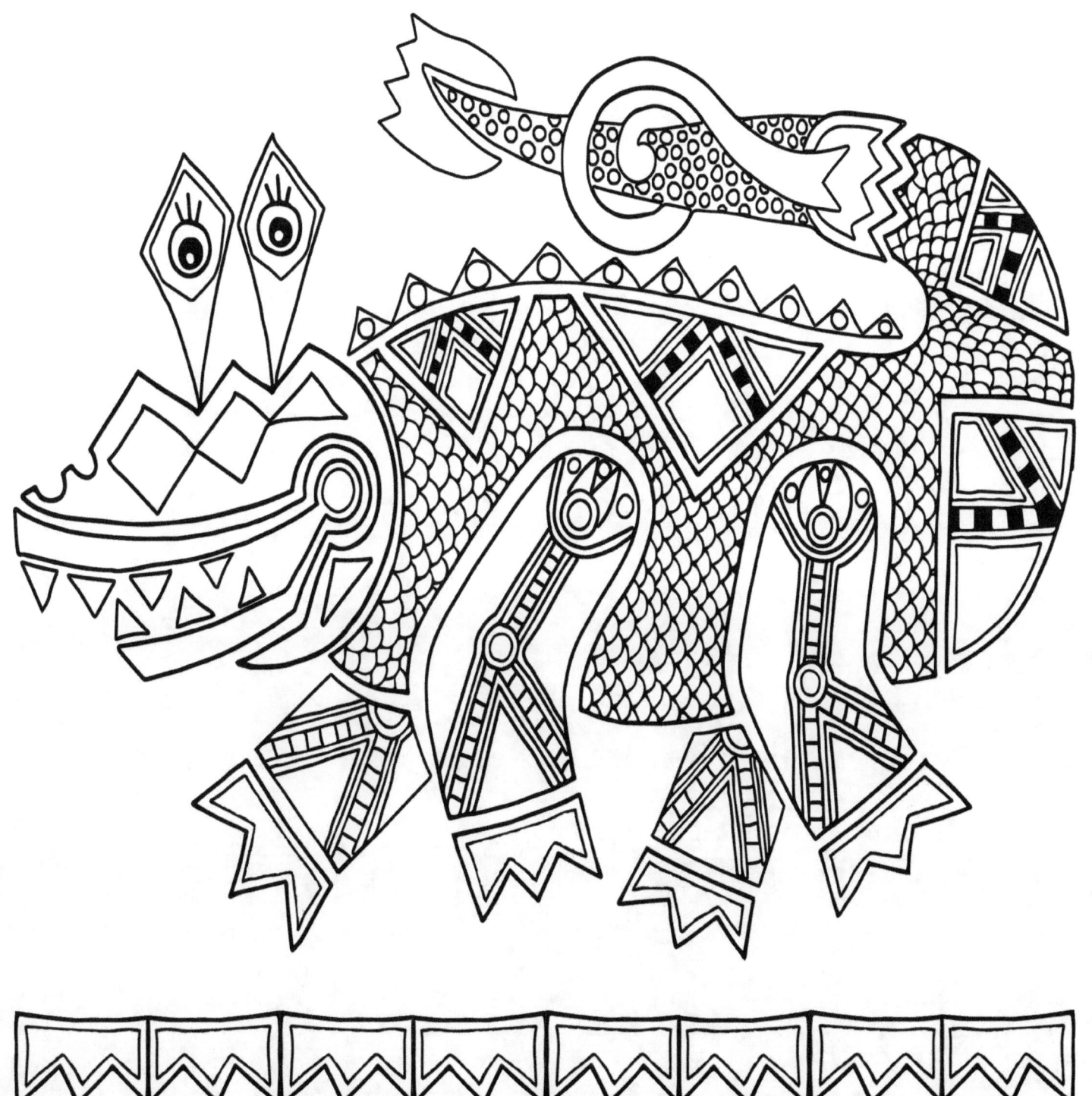

I SURROUND MYSELF WITH LOVING FRIENDS

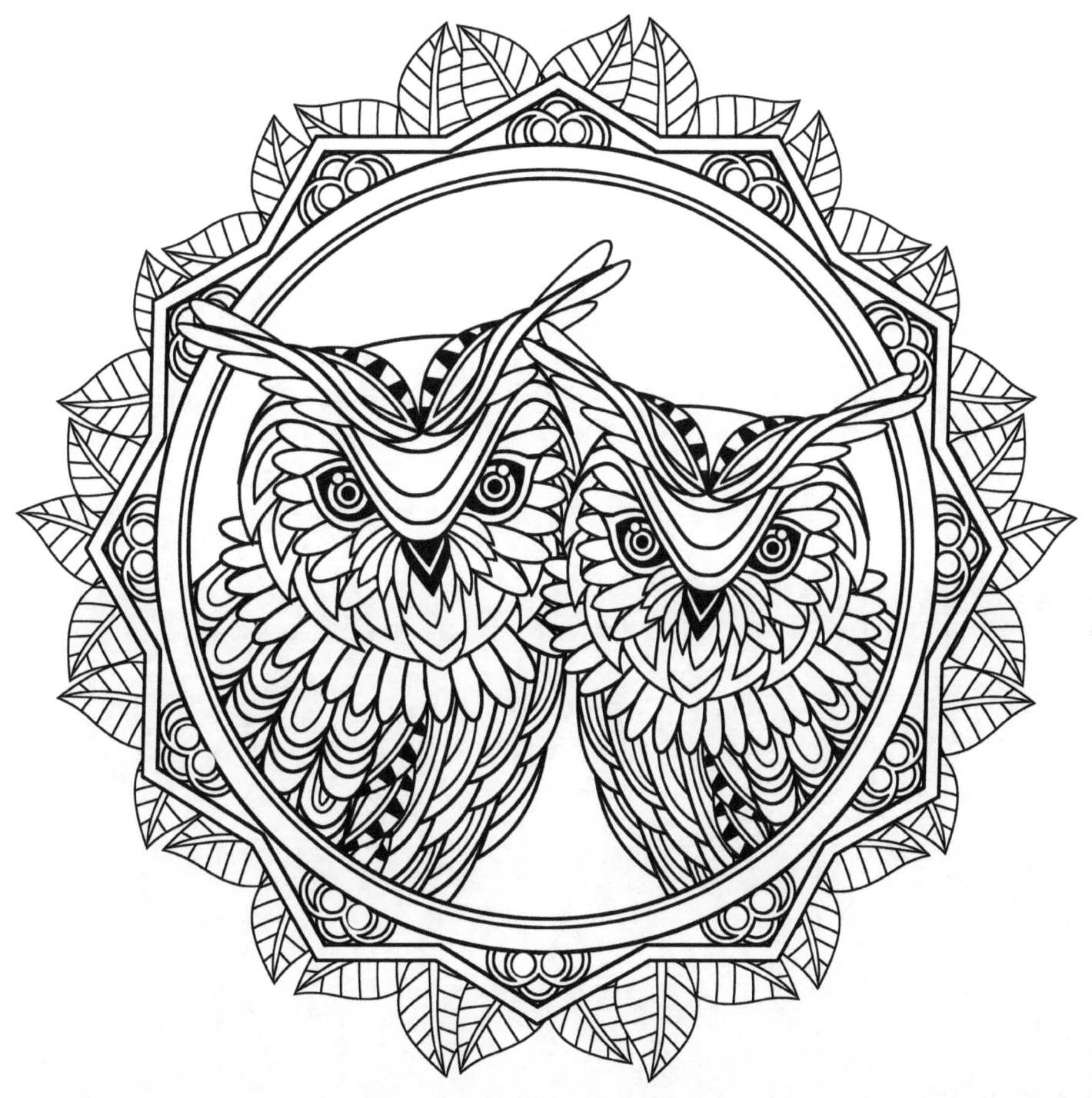

I MAKE ROOM FOR FUN

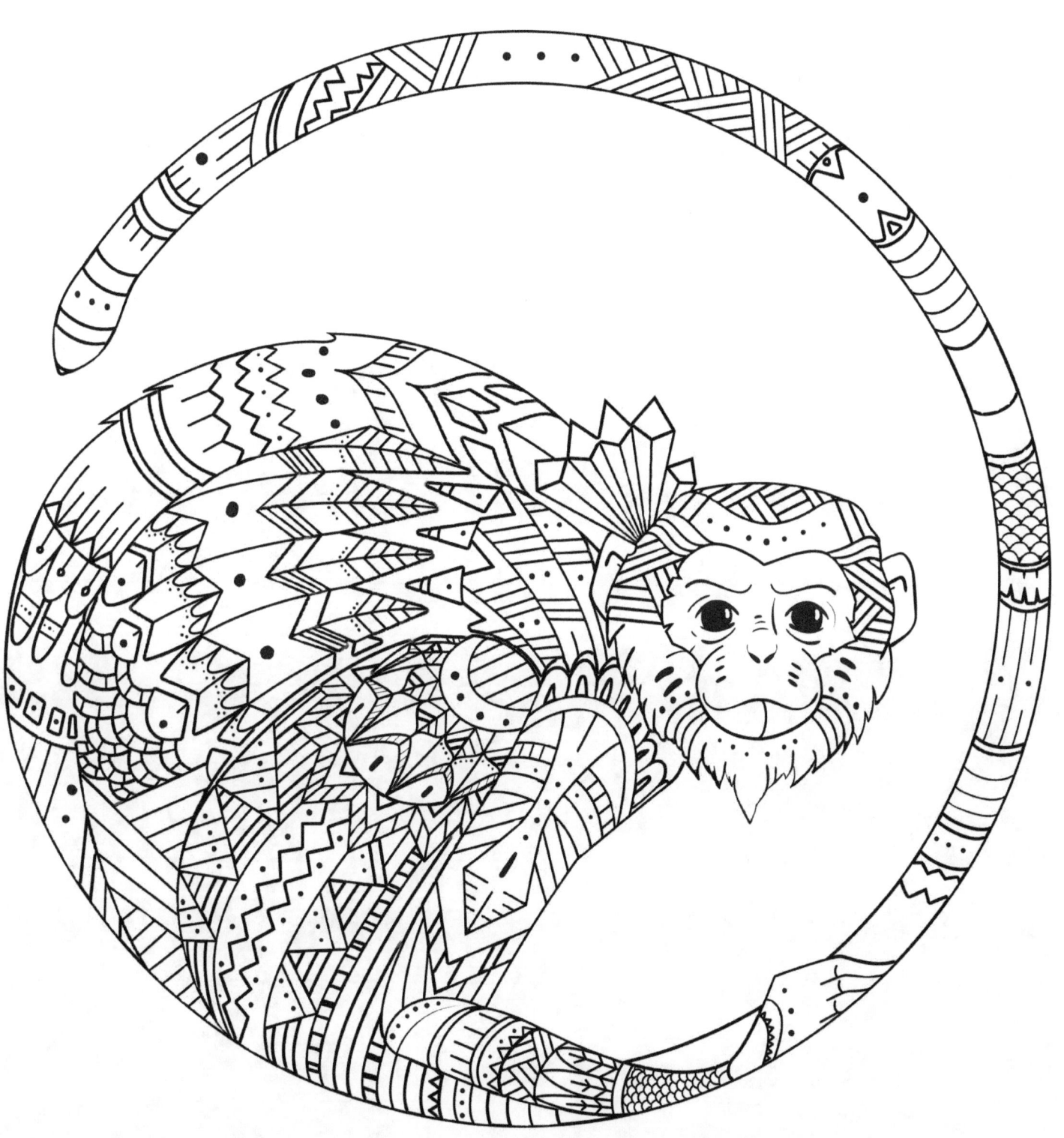

I WALK THE TALK

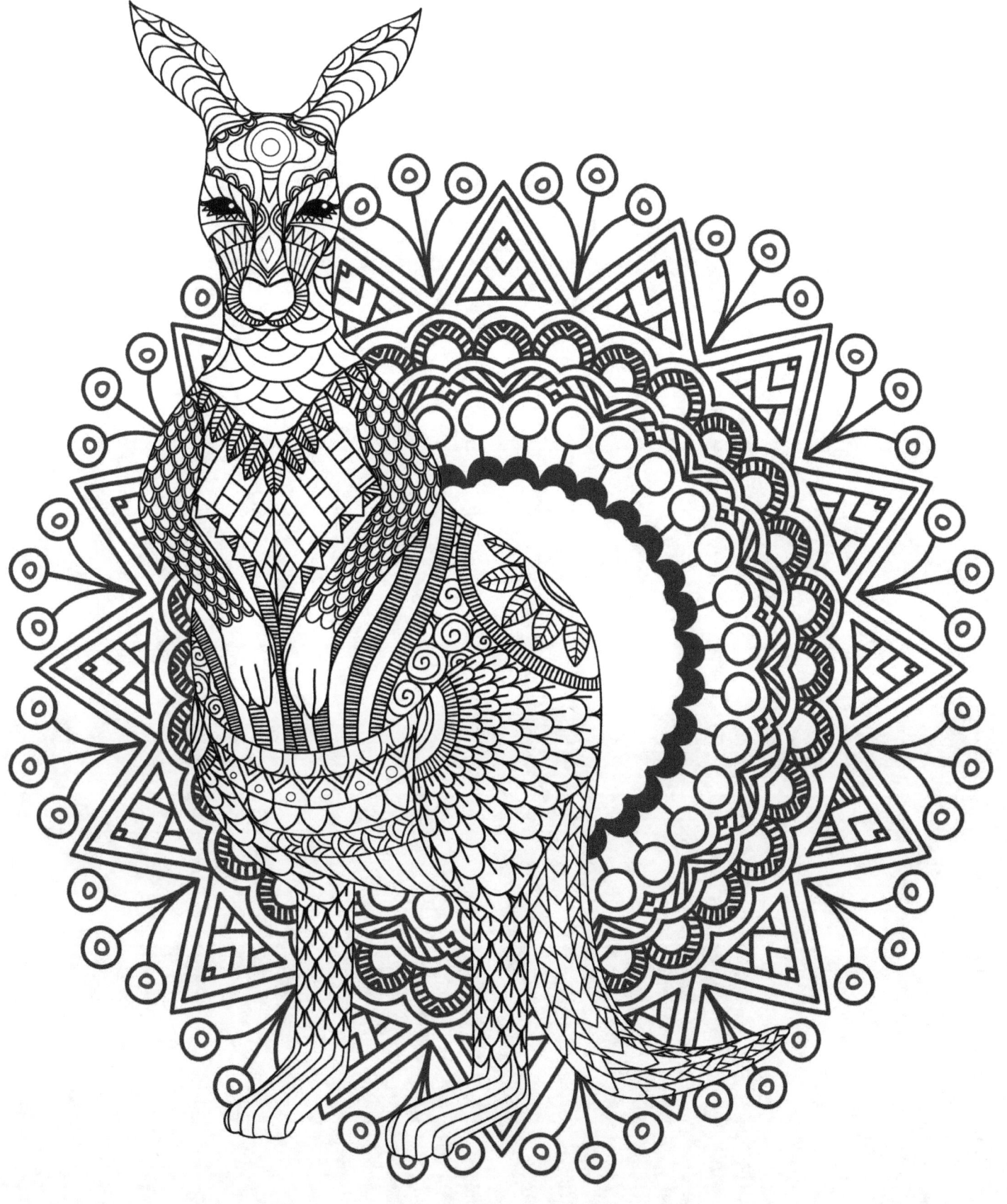

LIFE IS GREAT

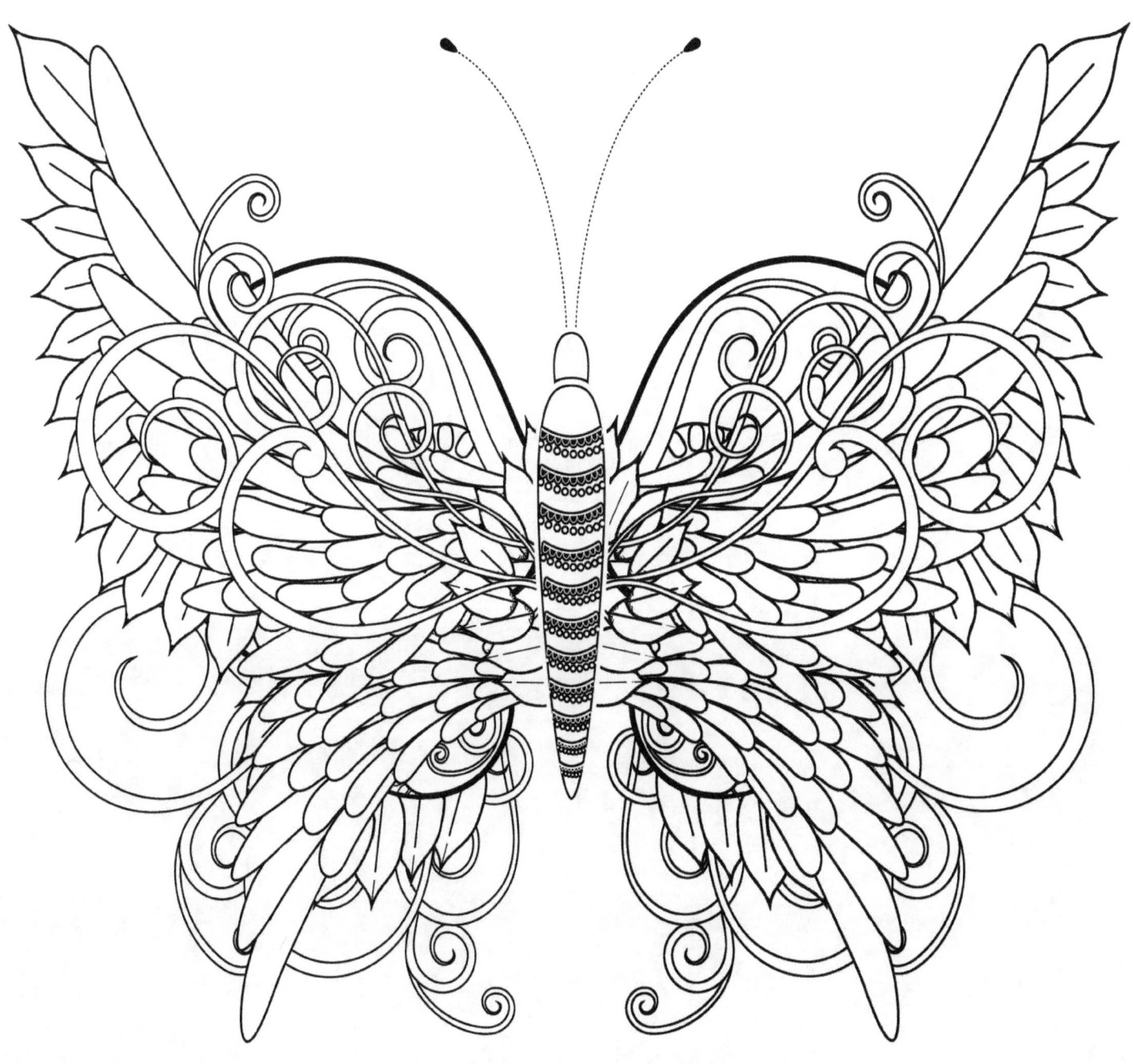

LOVE & GOODWILL SURROUND ME

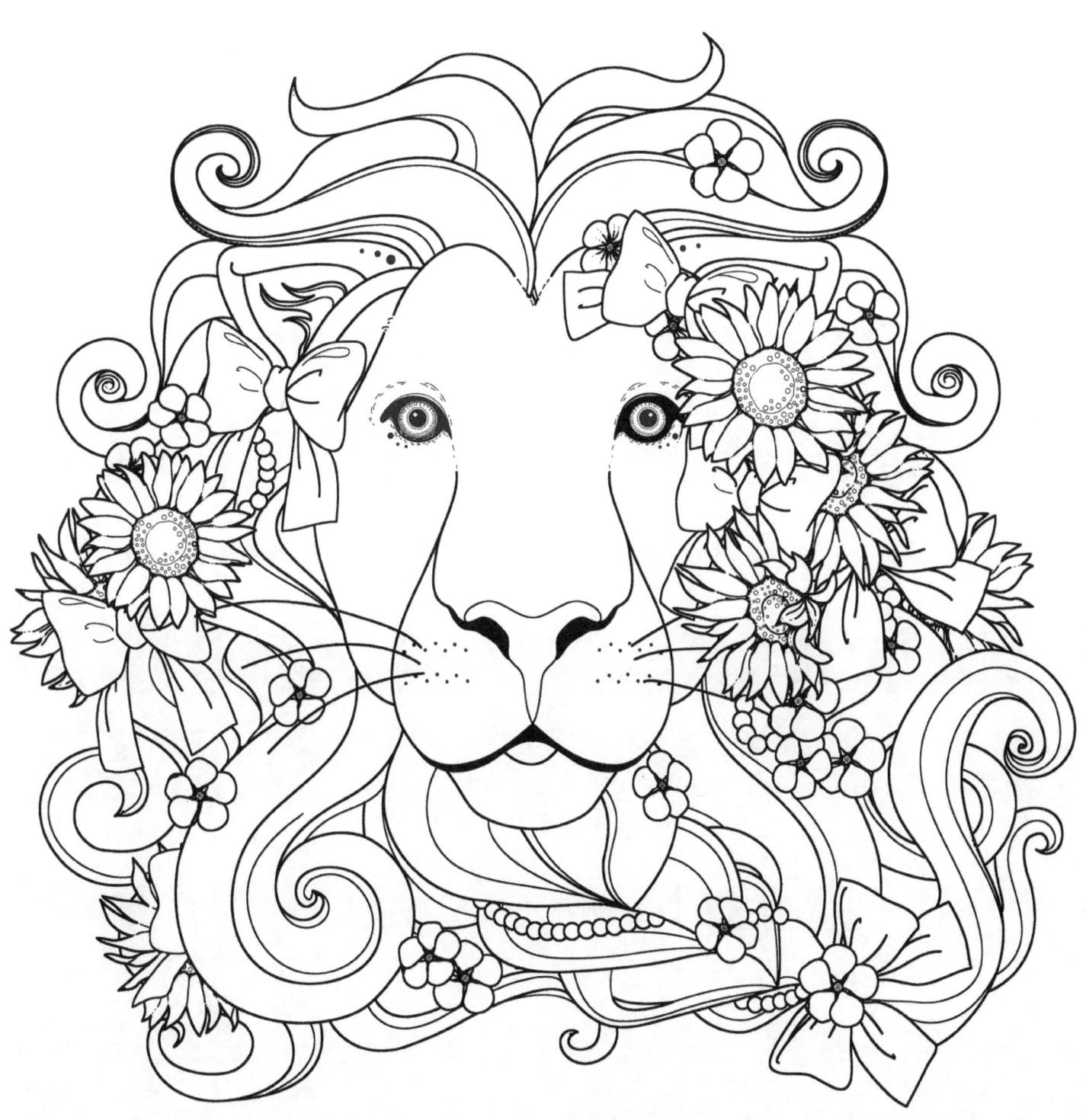

I STEP INTO THE WONDERFUL UNKNOWN

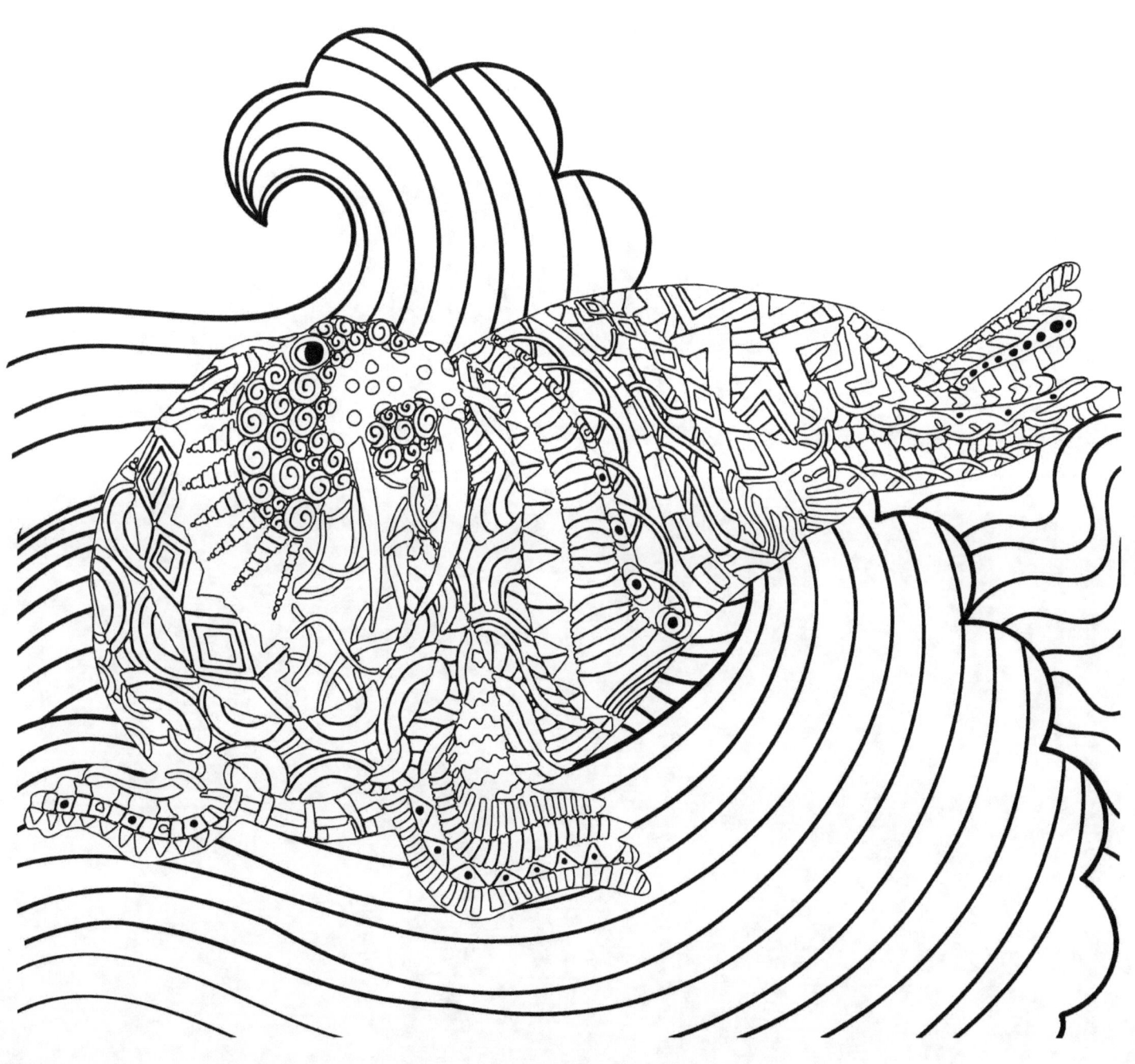

MY POWERFUL MOMENT IS NOW

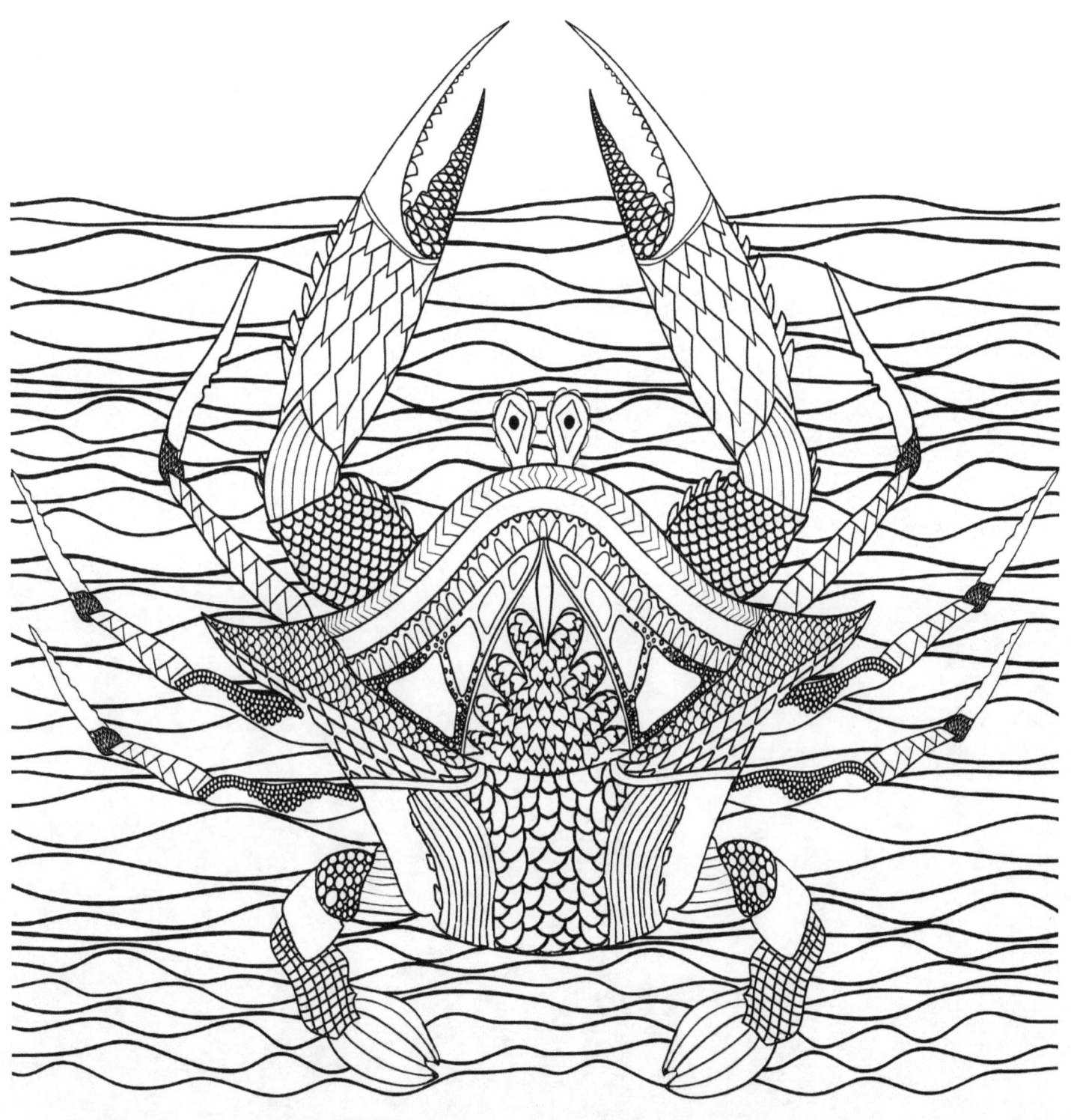

I LOVE WHERE I AM

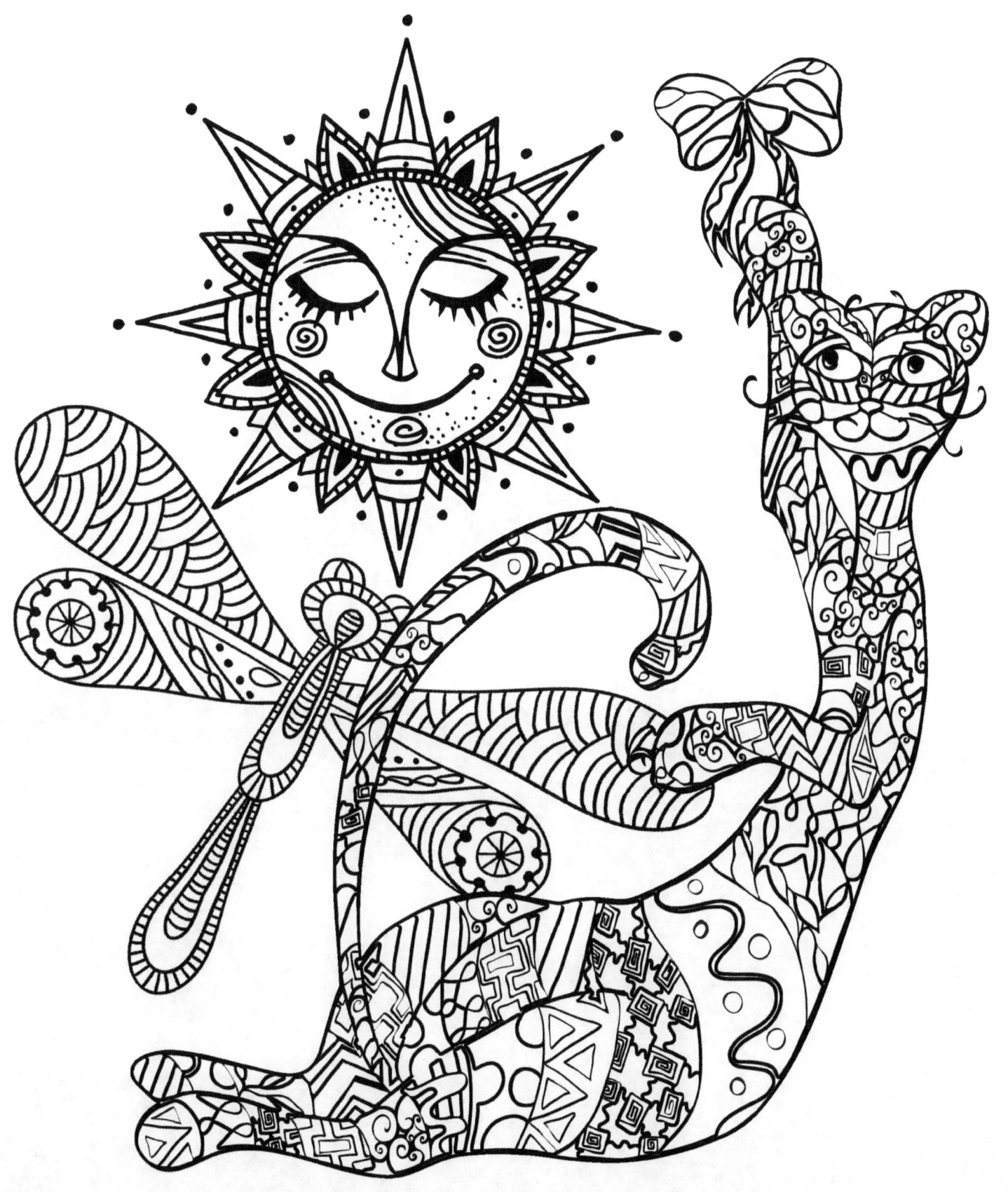

I AM GRATEFUL FOR BEING ME

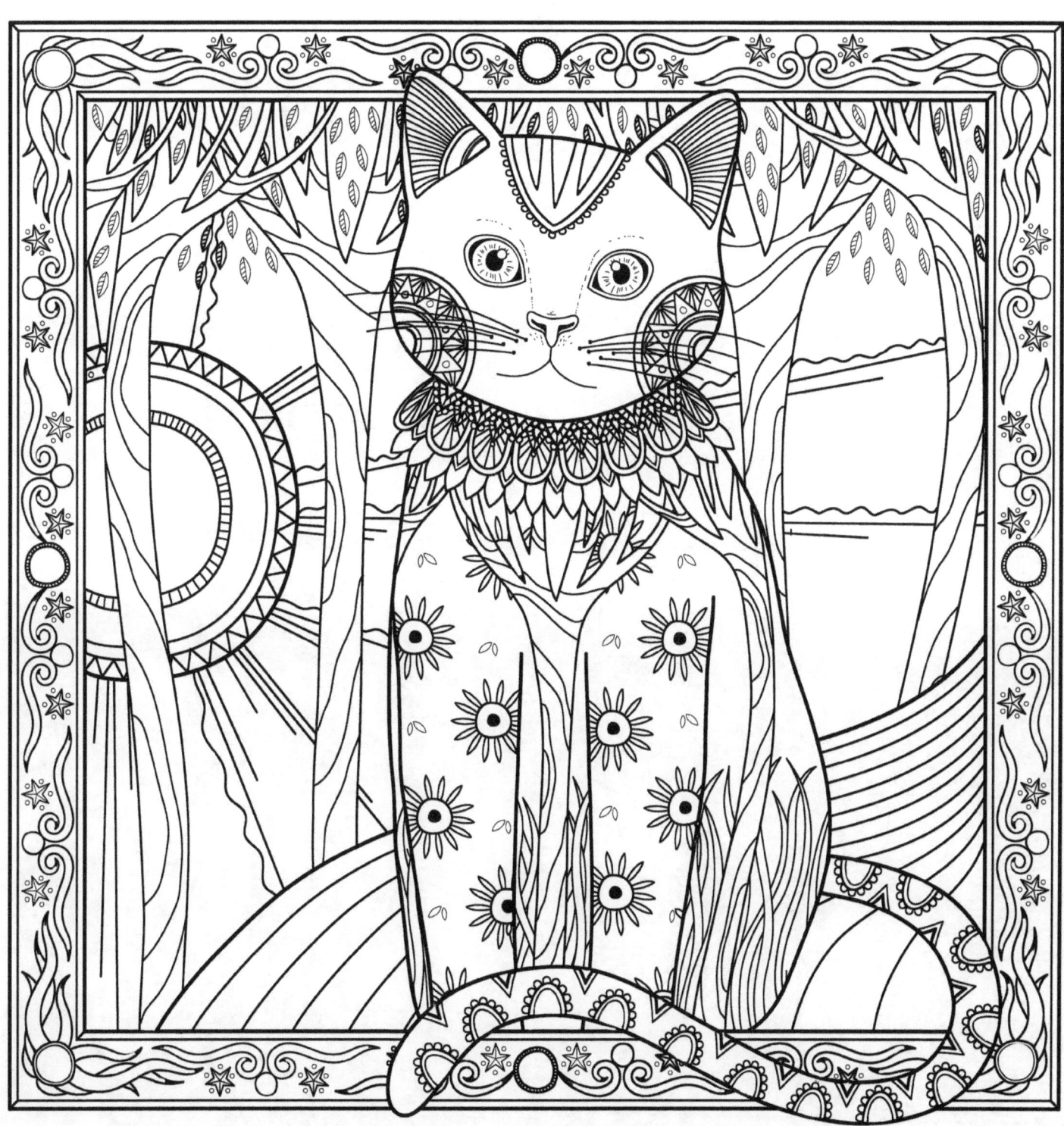

THANK YOU!

WE HOPE YOU HAD A WONDERFUL TIME coloring the fantastical animals in this collection and contemplating the uplifting affirmations that accompany them. It has been shown that positive thinking and repeating affirmative words each day can really help make our lives better. How much more effective must the effect be while accompanied by the imaginative flow of creating colorful artwork as you meditate upon them? Our hope is that this awesome zendala coloring book has provided you with hours of relaxation and stress-free artistic expression, engaged your imagination, and aroused your senses and creativity.

If you have a moment, please help others enjoy this book! Post a review online and tell them why you loved coloring this book!

MORE CREATIVE COLORING BOOKS FROM TRANSCENDENTAL COLORING GROUP:
Please visit: http://bit.ly/TransColor

Butterflies & Mandalas
Dragonflies & Mandalas
Pretty Shoes
Hummingbirds & Hamsas
My Big Bad Breakup
Creative Zendala Animals
Coloring for Book Lovers

PUBLISHED BY CAJUN HOT PRESS
CREATIVE ZENDALA ANIMALS: An Adult Coloring Book with Affirmations
ISBN-13:9781530770595
ISBN-10:1530770599 All rights reserved
Copyright © March 2016 by Cajun Hot Press, LLC

Cover art designed by Nina Bruhns.

Cajun Hot Press
March 2016

www.ingramcontent.com/pod-product-compliance
Lightning Source LLC
Chambersburg PA
CBHW080714190526
45169CB00006B/2369